BREAKTHROUGH IN ENGLISH:

NOVEL IDEAS

ANNE O'CATHASAIGH

Published 1985

© Anne O'Cathasaigh with Derek Wood 1985

ISBN 0 7231 0871 4

Published by University Tutorial Press Ltd, 842 Yeovil Road, Slough SL1 4JQ

Printed by Redwood Burn Ltd, Trowbridge, Wiltshire

CONTENTS

ACKNOWLEDGEMENTS

The author and publisher are grateful to the following for use of copyright material:

I had a Teenage Werewolf and other   Barry Norman
Home Movies
Looks and Smiles   Barry Hines   Michael Joseph Ltd.
The National Museum (Wales)   John Tripp by permission of the author, from *Second Aeon* Sphere
                                              Books
Maiden Name   Philip Larkin from *The Less Deceived* by permission of the Marvell
                                              Press
The Faithful Wife   Patricia Beer from *The Estuary* Macmillan, London and Basingstoke
Nervous Prostration   Anna Wickam *Selected Poems* by permission of the author's literary
                                              estate and Chatto & Windus
Sonnet XXXI   Edna St. Vincent Millay *Collected Poems* Harper & Row copyright 1923,
                                              1951 by Edna St. Vincent Millay & Norma Millay Ellis
The Shape of the Sword   Jorge Luis Borges from *Labyrinths* Penguin Books Ltd.
The Hero   Siegfried Sassoon by permission of George Sassoon
The Human Factor   Graham Greene from *The Human Factor* The Bodley Head
Marlon Brando   René Jordan from *Marlon Brando* W. H. Allen and Co. Ltd.
Visiting the Dead   Ciarán Carson from *The New Estate* Blackstaff Press Ltd.
Prayer Before Birth   Both from *Cadbury's First Book of Children's Poetry*
Mechanics
The Almond Tree   Jon Stallworthy from *Root and Branch* Chatto and Windus The Hogarth
                                              Press

The Little Girl and the Wolf James Thurber-collection Hamish Hamilton 1963 from *Vintage Thurber*

Bye Child Seamus Heaney from *Wintering Out* Faber and Faber Ltd

Ordinary Families E. Arnot Robertson by permission of David Higham Associates

The Bleeding Heart Marilyn French *The Bleeding Heart* André Deutsch

Flight Doris Lessing from *The Habit of Loving* Granada Publishing Ltd.

Footballers Don't Cry Brian Glanville – permission granted by John Farquharson Ltd. on behalf of the author

The Amazing Elephant Man M. Howell & P. Ford *The True History of the Elephant Man*

Images Of Ourselves; Women with Disabilities Talking Edited by Jo Campling, Routledge Kegan Paul PLC

Glasgow 5 March 1971 Edwin Morgan 1982 *Poems of Thirty Years* Carcanet New Press Manchester

To School with Fear Polly Davies from *Girls are Powerful* Sheba Feminist Press

The Collector John Fowles *The Collector* Jonathan Cape

The Guardian, John Ezard and Stephen Cook for permission to use:
On the New Beat in Brixton and *Seeing The Error of Their Ways*
The Sun for permission to use the following articles:
Belt Up Bates and *Jones Avoids Horror Injury*
The Sunday Times for permission to use the following:
Love Behind The Nissen Huts   Inside Rampton   A Life in the Day of Jack Jacobs
A Voice for the Young   Olly   Hello-Hello, Speak up Tiger & High Street Terror of the Shoplifting Gangs
The Observer for permission to use the following:
When Black Turns White and *The Problem That Doesn't Go Away*

Despite every effort by the publishers they have been unable to trace the authors of: *Patrick* and *Deborah and Mr. Jones.*

Thanks are due to the following for use of photographs:
p. 2, David Hoffman; pp. 6, 8, Barnaby's Picture Library; p. 7, George Williams; pp. 18, 28, 31, J. B. Briggs; p. 26, N.S.P.C.C.; p. 20, Mothercare; pp. 19, 46, 57, 85, Derek Wood; pp. 24, 28, George Williams Senior; p. 37, Janine Wiedel Picture Library; p. 29, Harvey Russell; 'Children of a Lesser God' p. 59 by courtesy of E&B Productions; 'The Elephant Man' p. 53 by courtesy of Thorn EMI Screen Entertainment; 'On the New Beat in Brixton' p. 82 by courtesy of the Metropolitan Police Force; 'Knights of the New York Subway' p. 69 by permission of Eve Arnold; Magnum p. 74 The Cambridge Photographers (Bob Seymore); p. 76, Sporting Pics; p. 29, Jeanette Hurworth

PREFACE

The theme of this resources book is the concept of Identity which is likely to be of personal interest to the student and also to be particularly useful in a country increasingly aware of minority groups within the community.

Chapter One looks beyond the stereotypes, of, for example, *The Teenager* or *The Wife*, so often presented in the media.

Chapter Two explores issues associated with growing up: for example parents' relationships with adolescent children and the complex situations which can arise within the family, such as how to bring up your child or how to cope with an ageing parent.

Chapter Three introduces the student to people who have not had an easy passage through life. It questions society's attitude to such outsiders.

Chapter Four presents different aspects of life in the world today: how do you react to the problem of bad housing, street violence or football hooliganism?

Each chapter will present the student with a selection of poems, prose passages, play extracts and newspaper articles. They are to be used as stimuli to prompt a strong response from the student, which will be expressed orally or in writing. After each extract a *Discussion or Writing* section follows with questions related to the passage and others which go on to probe the larger issues. Having to formulate your ideas in these ways will often lead to new insights into your feelings, attitudes and motives as regards your own experience of life.

While the focus is largely on creative writing and oral response consideration is also given to the technical skills expected of students. Each chapter contains:

a passage followed by traditional comprehension questions

a passage followed by multiple choice questions

a passage followed by a summary question

Specimen answers for the four comprehension and four multiple choice passages can be found at the back of the text.

In this book, *Breakthrough in English: Novel Ideas*, a wide range of topics is introduced by the extracts which were chosen for their punch, vigour and freshness.

Sincere thanks are to be given to Derek Wood, Head of Modern Languages, Meridian School, Royston, for the assistance he has given me from the book's conception and in particular for the compilation of questions for each Multiple Choice Passage.

I would also like to thank the members of the English Department, Meridian School, Royston, who tested the work with their classes and reported back to me their impressions. This was an invaluable help. Adele Abbott, librarian at the Meridian School, must be thanked for all the typing she did and for her patience and enthusiasm.

Anne O'Cathasaigh

IDENTITY

I HAD A TEENAGE WEREWOLF AND OTHER HOME MOVIES

There is a film going the rounds which begins with the assumption that America has been infested by a group of zombies. What they have done, these zombies, is they've risen somewhat unexpectedly from the grave and, in search of sustenance, taken to biting chunks out of non-zombies, presumably in an attempt to keep body and soul apart.

Now give or take a certain greyish pallor and a marked tendency towards redness around the eyes they look pretty well like everybody else and, in fact, don't do very much except moon aimlessly about, rather like secondary pickets.

Well, I won't go into an analysis of the film but what struck me about it was that at no time was any explanation offered for the presence of the said zombies. They were simply there, take them or leave them. This, said the movie, in effect, is America and America has zombies. Don't ask why, it just does.

And I was thinking how preposterous this was and arguing that nothing simply appears without explanation when it dawned on me that a similar phenomenon had occurred in my own midst and, indeed, in the midst of most of my friends.

I don't mean we've been infested with zombies – no such luck. We've been afflicted with something far worse – teenagers. And like the zombies in the movie they suddenly appeared, just like that, from nowhere.

Not so long ago, as I recall, we all had perfectly charming and biddable children whose parents' word was law. And then one morning they all rose up from their beds like the living dead and revealed the dreadful fact that they had been transmogrified into teenagers.

Like zombies – and secondary pickets – teenagers don't seem much different from anybody else, give or take, in the case of females, a certain greyish pallor and a marked tendency towards heavy blackness around the eyes (all self-inflicted with the aid of cosmetics) and in the case of males, a less greyish pallor and a marked tendency towards pimples everywhere.

And again like zombies and secondary pickets they moon around aimlessly. True they don't – not yet anyway – rip lumps of flesh off their traditional enemy, the non-teenager or easygoing parent, but I suspect

that it will come because, from the start, they all show a definite inclination to bite the hand that feeds them.

The teenager is a creature of prey. On the floor of its bedroom it makes an ill-constructed nest out of its own discarded clothing – last week's jeans, trousers, skirts, sweaters, shirts, underwear etc. – because the teenager has lost the power to bend and pick anything up with its hands. And from the midst of this nest its threatening cry is heard by day and night. 'Gimme, gimme, gimme' it cries with a fearful scowl.

The easygoing parent ignores this cry at its peril because what the teenager isn't given it takes.

Regardless of sex it takes your clothes. For instance, it sweeps into your bedroom in the early morning shouting, 'Oh God, you haven't washed my favourite sweater yet and I left it specially on the floor for you as long ago as last night.' And then without so much as a by your leave, it descends upon your chest of drawers and rummages through the contents, hurling them around the room, until it comes across something that takes its fancy and, with a hoarse growl, carries it off to its filthy lair.

The teenager has a particular penchant for socks – other people's socks. It wears them under calf length boots and so doesn't mind wearing odd socks so that when it's finished its foul work the easygoing parent is reduced to perming any two from a selection of one brown, one grey, one black and one blue sock.

Furthermore the teenager is torpid by day – especially when there's anything resembling work to be done – and frenetic by night, when it insists on prowling far afield.

Unhappily, it is incapable of conveying itself from point A to point B unless it is taken there and back in its parents' car and, because it hates travelling alone, at least eight of its friends have to be collected from far-flung parts of the county.

Any nervous attempt at conversation by the ferrying parent is inevitably ignored by the assembled teenagers or, at best, answered with contemptuous grunts.

Arrived at point B the original teenager demands money with menaces and vanishes into the night with a surly warning that it will phone (reversing the charges of course) when it wishes to be collected.

Whereupon the parent drives desperately away to snatch a few moments of blissful peace, thanking God that just for once these ruthless plunderers are going to tear someone else's home apart. There is but one consolation: close acquaintance with teenagers has divested me of any fear I might have had of flesh-eating zombies. Indeed if you replaced my resident teenagers with flesh-eating zombies I don't think I'd notice the difference.

Barry Norman
THE GUARDIAN

*I HAD A TEENAGE WEREWOLF
AND OTHER HOME MOVIES*
FOR DISCUSSION OR WRITING

1 Do you recognise yourself in any of the criticisms Barry Norman levels at teenagers?
2 Do you think you react differently to your parents now that you are older?
3 Write an essay putting forward your criticisms of parents' behaviour.
4 An argument has arisen between a parent and child. Give two different accounts of the argument, from the parent's and the child's point of view. You might like to write these as diary entries.

DEBORAH
AND MR JONES

As you read the following conversation between Mr. Jones, an English teacher, and a fifth year pupil, Deborah, ask yourself how Deborah 'prepares a face' for her teacher. The parts written in parenthesis are her thoughts.

Mr. Jones is a little disappointed with my MCT questions results in the Mock 'O' Level.

'This is grade 'B' – but you will be aiming for an 'A' next year?'

(Don't change facial expression – give nothing away.)

'Yes, Mr. Jones.'

(For God's sake what do you think I am – infallible? Just because I can write he's disappointed because I only got a grade 'B' in his poxy exam. Go to Hell. I don't live up to other people's standards. I live up to mine.)

'Those MCT questions – I know the exam room was noisy – you seemed to lose concentration at intervals.'

(Stare out of the window, appear disinterested. No reply. Let him think what he wants. I didn't lose concentration. I did my utmost best with those questions, but it wasn't good enough, was it? They were bloody difficult and I'm not the genius you think I am. You need common sense and the powers of intricate deduction to answer questions like that. And I don't happen to possess those powers – so sorry – I fell a little short of your expectations, didn't I?)

'This essay is good – but you didn't manage to finish it – you lost marks for that, you'll have to learn the art of finishing things. Do you think you'll manage to do that next year? – I know it's against your principles but....'

'No.'

(Nothing dramatic, don't look at him. Remain aloof. Of course it's against my principles. I'm a writer not a bloody automaton. Does he think I can sit down and churn out a polished grade 'A' essay, finished mind you, finished in forty-five minutes? I write what I want and when I have something to say. Anything else is third rate, boring, unfinished and unoriginal. I don't know what you're complaining about. Grade 'B' is brilliant, considering that under exam conditions I'm no better than the average candidate. I can't switch on this ability of mine, y'know. It comes and goes. I wrote nothing for about four months, remember? Everything just went. It's just about coming back now – but I'm not in control. I'M NOT IN CONTROL.)

'Well you really shouldn't have tackled a story that you get too deeply into – perhaps a description would have suited you better – something you could have finished?'

Short silence. (What, does he want me to say something? Perhaps ask him where I went wrong? Advice on how not to get a grade 'B' in your mock 'O' level? Don't you see? I don't care, I don't give a damn about what grade I get? I don't care if it's the lowest possible pass. I don't care if it's CSE. Just so long as I've got those stupid bits of paper to wave under an employer's nose. I've already got enough people arranging my life for me – I don't need another. And especially not you. I would have expected it from anyone but you.)

'Here you are then.'

'What, have I got to keep it?'

(All non-commital stuff this)

'Yes, a present for you.'

(Thanks for nothing.)

'Thank you.'

DEBORAH AND MR JONES
FOR DISCUSSION OR WRITING

1 Do you adopt different roles with different people? If you do, give examples of the different faces you present.
2 Rewrite the conversation between Deborah and Mr. Jones including Mr. Jones' thoughts.
3 Do you sympathise with Deborah's views on examinations?
4 Writing to order – do you find this a difficult task?

LOOKS
AND SMILES

The Social Security office was crowded. The rows of chairs at the back of the room were all occupied and there were five long queues at the counter. Some of the adults had brought their children with them and the crying of babies and the persistent whining of bored toddlers made the atmosphere fractious.

There was even a dog in the place: a lean black mongrel that had wandered in by mistake and was now going peacefully about its business, sniffing around and cocking its leg against the furniture. Nobody took any notice of it, they had too much to worry about to care about a stray dog, until a little girl grabbed its tail and it spun round snarling and baring its teeth. This gave those near the incident an excuse to relieve some of their frustrations, and they shouted at the dog and kicked out at it. The dog scuffled across the room, skidding a little on the vinyl tiles, but still managing to dodge the flying feet without much difficulty. It had had a lot of practice avoiding kicks in its travels around the city.

When it had gone, everybody turned back to the front and settled down in their queues again. There were five queues formed up in front of the five lettered boards hanging above the counter. Mick was in queue E because his surname began with one of the last letters of the alphabet.

There was another diversion when an argument developed at the front of queue C. A man was accusing the clerk of not sending his claims in on time, which meant his Giro cheques were arriving late. The clerk said that he didn't know anything about it. As far as he knew, his claims went through like everybody else's. The man said he had four children to support and the clerk replied that that had nothing to do with him. The man told him not to be so bloody clever and called him a jumped-up pen-pusher. The clerk said it was no good blaming him. He was just doing his job. Eventually, the man signed his coupon and walked away, still abusing the clerk as he made for the door. He kicked over an ashtray on a metal stand and, as it fell, it hit a little boy on the leg and made him cry. There was another row then between the disgruntled claimant and the little boy's mother.

There was no trouble when Mick reached the front of the queue. He smiled at the girl as he passed his registration card across the counter, but she ignored him and began to search quickly for his claim-unit in a filing tray at her side. Mick stared at the top of her head, willing her to look up at him so that he could say something to her; something witty that would make her laugh. But she took no notice of him. She had no time for badinage. There were a lot of people behind Mick and they were in no mood for unnecessary delays. As she passed his claim form to fill in, Mick noticed that she was wearing an engagement ring. Miserable cow, he thought. He was glad she wasn't getting married to him.

Mick signed the form: Michael Walsh. It looked incomplete without his class after it, 5G2. But this wasn't a new exercise book, or a school examination paper. All that was behind him now. He was signing on the dole.

After he had left the Social Security office, Mick went to meet his friends in Woolworths. They hadn't arranged a time because they usually spent all morning there when they came to town. It was the best place they knew. It was warm. They could sit in the cafeteria for hours for the price of a cup of tea, or they could just wander through the departments testing the goods. In 'Toiletries', they squirted each other with hairspray and deodorants. From the confectionary displays they sampled the occasional sweet, and in the electrical department they switched the television sets on and off with remote-control panels, when *genuine* customers were trying to choose.

It was easy, because it was nearly all self-service now. The shop had been refitted, the staff reduced, and the old sections, with half a dozen girls behind each stall, had disappeared.

Mick found Alan and Steve in the music department. Steve was arguing with the assistant because she wouldn't put a record on for him. He kept showing her the cover and she kept shaking her head.

'No, I'm not playing you any more.'

'Why not? I might want to buy it.'

'You've no intention of buying it. Anyway, I've played you three already.'

'So what? That's what you're paid for, isn't it?' She snatched the cover from him and put it down behind the counter.

'Don't be cheeky.' She wasn't much older than Steve, but being in work gave her the authority. 'And you can clear off. Hanging around here all day. It's a pity you've nothing else to do with your time.' Steve looked at the price of the album he would like to have bought.

'We haven't. That's the trouble.'

While Steve was arguing with the assistant, Mick and Alan walked across to a display of electronic organs. Alan plugged one in and Mick played the opening bars of Handel's Wedding March on it. The other customers looked startled, then amused, but they did not have the opportunity to hear any more of Mick's recital, because the assistant from the record counter rushed across and pulled out the plug. Grinning at her, Mick continued to play, even though no notes came from the depressed keys. This made the harrassed assistant even more angry.

'Look, get off it! You'll be breaking it, messing about like that.'

'Messing about!' Alan was outraged at this assessment of Mick's performance. 'He used to play the organ in church, him, you know.'

Steve looked up from the records.

'Ar, that one under his cassock.'

And the accompanying gesture with his right hand made the assistant blush.

'You dirty devil.'

But as she walked back behind the counter she had to try hard not to smile. The boys laughed and walked away.

They went upstairs for a cup of tea, then Steve said that he had to go and meet his dad, who knew somebody who might be able to find him a job. Mick and Alan decided that they ought to go job-hunting too. They left Steve at the door of the shop, then went off together to look for a telephone box.

Barry Hines

LOOKS AND SMILES
FOR DISCUSSION OR WRITING

1 To pass the time, Mick and his friends 'clown around' in Woolworths. Why do you think they behave like this?
2 Do you believe that most people have a vocation in life?
3 Is job satisfaction important?
4 What are your own views about 'signing on the dole'?
5 Do you worry about the possibility that when you leave school you might not find a job?

LEISURE ACTIVITIES

LEISURE ACTIVITIES
FOR DISCUSSION OR WRITING

1 Imagine the boy fishing in 'Leisure Activities' is unemployed. Write an interior monologue showing his thoughts, contrasting the present moment with his fears for the future.
2 In the photograph 'Leisure Activities' we see two different types of pastimes. What do you enjoy doing in your spare time?

IN THE NATIONAL MUSEUM (WALES)

I went there on Tuesdays
At lunchtime, to look
At the Impressionists. Their colours
Could take me into an old French summer
5 And let Cardiff sink in the Taff.
I never told her I went there
Because she despised arty men.
Outside, at the top of the steps,
I took off my deerstalker
10 And hid my sandwich tin behind a pillar.
Inside, under the big dome and high balcony,
There was dignity in the marble hush.
I adjusted my steel-rimmed specs
For the feast ahead. Then I saw the back of her
15 With an arm through some man's
Going up the wide stairs. I turned back

To the revolving doors, scared,
Thinking I would strangle her later.
She was wearing her best dress
20 And her hair was like flame.

John Tripp

IN THE NATIONAL MUSEUM (WALES)
FOR DISCUSSION OR WRITING

1 Continue the story.
2 Write about a similar situation you have experienced, when you felt extremely jealous owing to another person's actions.
3 Write a poem entitled 'Poisoned Love'.

MAIDEN NAME

Marrying left your maiden name disused.
Its five light sounds no longer mean your face,
Your voice, and all your variants of grace;
For since you were so thankfully confused
5 By law with someone else, you cannot be
Semantically the same as that young beauty:
It was of her that these two words were used.

Now it's a phrase, applicable to no one,
Lying just where you left it, scattered through
10 Old lists, old programmes, a school prize or two,
Packets of letters tied with a tartan ribbon –
Then is it scentless, weightless, strengthless, wholly
Untruthful? Try whispering it slowly.
No it means you. Or, since you're past and gone,

15 It means that what we feel about you then:
How beautiful you were and near, and young,
So vivid, you might still be there among
Those first few days, unfingermarked again.
So your old name shelters our faithfulness,
20 Instead of losing shape and meaning less
With your depreciating luggage laden.

Philip Larkin

MAIDEN NAME
FOR DISCUSSION OR WRITING

1 Does marriage necessarily mean that one's identity is 'confused' with one's partner's?
2 Do you think a woman should adopt her husband's surname?
3 Do you consider it sentimental to keep photographs, love letters and other such mementoes? Why do people treasure these things? Do you?

THE KISS
FOR DISCUSSION OR WRITING

1 'The Kiss' shows two people who are close but yet apart. Is a good marriage one in which each partner feels secure yet has enough room to grow and develop?
2 Do you think that marriage is an old-fashioned 'institution'?
3 Assess the case for getting married at a young age (sixteen to nineteen) or delaying until one is more mature.

THE FAITHFUL WIFE

I am away from home
A hundred miles from the blue curtains
I made at Christmas and the table
My grandfather brought back from Sorrento.
5 I am a career woman at a conference.
I love my husband. I value
Both what I own and what I do.

I left the forsythia half yellow,
The bluebells – lifted from a wood in Suffolk
10 Last year – still tight, the mint surfacing.
I must sweep the paths when I get back.
And here for the past week you and I
Have been conducting a non-affair
That could not even be called flirtation
15 That could not be called anything
Except unusually straightforward desire,
Adultery in the heart.
Life is so short.

The programme is ending.
20 11.30 – Conference disperses.
I watch everybody leaving.
It feels like grief, like the guillotine.

You turn now: go home
With the 'Good-bye, love'
25 You use to every personable woman.
Get in your large car which ten years ago
Was full of sand and children's things
On summer evenings.

You are middle-aged now, as I am.
30 Write your notes up,
Fix the rattling window,
Keep your marriage vows. As I shall.

Patricia Beer

**THE FAITHFUL WIFE
FOR DISCUSSION OR WRITING**

1 Is this woman guilty of infidelity for having wanted to have an affair with the middle-aged man she met at a conference, even though she didn't?
2 You are walking down the street and the man in front of you drops five pounds unknowingly. You pick it up and intend to slip it into your own pocket, but realise several other people have seen the whole incident. You run after the man and give him his money. Are you guilty of theft, for having intended to keep the money, although you did return it?
3 Is an unfulfilled impulse to be unfaithful or dishonest as bad as the actual act? Could one sometimes gain from the experience in some way?

NERVOUS PROSTRATION

I married a man of the Croydon class
When I was twenty-two.
And I vex him, and he bores me
Till we don't know what to do!
5 It isn't good form in the Croydon class
To say you love your wife,
So I spend my days with the tradesmen's books
And pray for the end of life.

In green fields are blossoming trees
10 And a golden wreath of gorse,
And young birds sing for joy of worms:
It's perfectly clear of course,
That it wouldn't be taste in the Croydon class

To sing over dinner or tea:
15 But I sometimes wish the gentleman
Would turn and talk to me!

But every man of the Croydon class
Lives in terror of joy and speech.
'Words are betrayers,' 'Joys are brief' –
20 The maxims their wise ones teach –
And for all my labour of love and life
I shall be clothed and fed,
And they'll give me an orderly funeral
When I'm still enough to be dead.

Anna Wickham
(1884–1947)

Oh, oh you will be sorry for that word!
Give back my book and take my kiss instead.
Was it my enemy or my friend I heard,
'What a big book for such a little head!'
5 'Come, I will show you my newest hat,
And you may watch me purse my mouth and prink!
Oh, I shall love you still, and all of that.
I never again shall tell you what I think.
I shall be sweet and crafty, soft and sly;
10 You will not catch me reading any more:
I shall be called a wife to pattern by;
And some day when you knock and push the door,
Some sane day, not too bright and not too stormy,
I shall be gone, and you may whistle for me.

Edna St. Vincent Millay
(1892–1950)

NERVOUS PROSTRATION AND SONNET XXXI
FOR DISCUSSION OR WRITING

1 Do you feel sorry for these women and their experience of married life?

2 Do men still feel superior to women intellectually or do you think that this is an out-dated stance?

3 From your own experience do you feel that there is equality between the sexes?

4 What is your opinion of the cliché 'A woman's place is in the home'? Should a man ever be the one to stay at home and take charge of household affairs?

5

Man	Woman
Be a man	Be a woman
If you can can	Be a wife
Walk tall	Someone's daughter
So they call	Someone's girlfriend
You superman	All your life

Are these stereotypes recognisable from programmes on television, stories in magazines or indeed from real life? Do you think that boys are brought up to be aggressive while girls are trained to be passive? Would you differentiate between your children in this way?

THE SHAPE OF
THE SWORD

A spiteful scar crossed his face: an ash-coloured and nearly perfect arc that creased his temple at one tip and his cheek at the other. His real name is of no importance: everyone in Tacaurembo called him 'The 5 Englishman from La Colorada'. Cardoso, the owner of those fields, refused to sell them: I understand that the Englishman resorted to an unexpected argument: he confided to Cardoso the secret of the scar. The Englishman came from the border, from Rio Grande 10 del Sur; there are many who say that in Brazil he had been a smuggler. The fields were overgrown with grass, the water-holes brackish; the Englishman, in order to correct those deficiencies, worked fully as hard as his labourers. They say that he was severe to 15 the point of cruelty, but scrupulously just. They say also that he drank: a few times a year he locked himself into an upper room, not to emerge until two or three days later as if from a battle or from vertigo, pale, trembling, confused and as authoritarian as ever. I remember his 20 glacial eyes, the energetic leanness, the grey moustache. He had no dealings with anyone; it is a fact that his Spanish was rudimentary and cluttered with Brazilian. Aside from a business letter or some pamphlet he received no mail. 25 The last time I passed through the northern provinces, a sudden overflowing of the Caraguata stream compelled me to spend the night at La Colorada. Within a few moments, I seemed to sense that my appearance was inopportune; I tried to ingratiate 30 myself with the Englishman; I resorted to the least discerning of passions: patriotism. I claimed as invincible a country with such spirit as England's. My companion agreed, but added with a smile that he was not English. He was Irish, from Dungarvan. Having said this, he stopped short, as if he had revealed a secret.

After dinner, we went outside to look at the sky. It had cleared up but beyond the low hills the southern sky, streaked and gashed by lightning, was conceiving another storm. Into the cleared-up dining-room the boy who had served dinner brought a bottle of rum. We drank for some time, in silence.

I don't know what time it must have been when I observed that I was drunk; I don't know what inspiration or what exultation or tedium made me mention the scar. The Englishman's face changed expression; for a few seconds I thought he was going to throw me out of the house. At length he said in his normal voice: 'I'll tell you the history of my scar under one condition: that of not mitigating one bit of the opprobrium, of the infamous circumstances.' I agreed. This is the story that he told me, mixing his English with Spanish, and even with Portuguese:

'Around 1922, in one of the battles of Connaught, I was one of the many who were conspiring for the independence of Ireland. Of my comrades, some are still living, dedicated to peaceful pursuits; others, paradoxically are fighting on desert and sea under the British flag; another, the most worthy, died in the courtyard of a barracks, at dawn, shot by men filled with sleep; still others (not the most fortunate) met their destiny in the anonymous and most secret battles of the civil war. We were Republicans, Catholics; we were, I suspect, romantics. One afternoon I will never forget an affiliate from Munster joined us: one John Vincent Moon.

'He was scarcely twenty years old. He was slender and flaccid at the same time; he gave the uncomfortable impression of being invertebrate. He had studied with fervour and with vanity nearly every page of Lord knows what Communist manual; he made use of dialectical materialism to put an end to any discussion whatever. The reasons one can have for hating another man, or for loving him, are infinite: Moon reduced the history of the Universe to a sordid economic conflict. He affirmed that the revolution was predestined to succeed. I told him that for a gentleman only lost causes should be attractive... Night had already fallen: we continued our disagreement in the hall, on the stairs, then along the vague streets. The judgements Moon emitted impressed me less than his irrefutable, apodictic[1] note. The new comrade did not discuss; he dictated opinions with scorn and with a certain anger. As we were arriving at the outlying houses, a sudden burst of gunfire stunned us. (Either before or afterwards we skirted the blank wall of a factory or barracks.) We moved into an unpaved street; a soldier, huge in the firelight, came out of a burning hut. Crying out, he ordered us to stop. I quickened my pace; my companion did not follow. I turned around: John Vincent Moon was motionless, fascinated, as if eternized by fear. I then ran back and knocked the soldier to the ground with one blow, shook Vincent Moon, insulted him and ordered him to follow. I had to take him by the arm; the passion of fear had rendered him helpless. We fled, into the night pierced by flames. A rifle volley reached out for us, and a bullet nicked Moon's right shoulder; as we were fleeing amid pines, he broke out in a weak sobbing.

'In that fall of 1923 I had taken shelter in General Berkeley's country house. The General (whom I had never seen) was carrying out some administrative assignment or other in Bengal; the house was less than a century old, but it was decayed and shadowy and flourished in puzzling corridors and in pointless antechambers. The museum and huge library usurped the first floor: controversial and uncongenial books which in some manner are the history of the nineteenth century; scimitars from Nishapur, along whose captured arcs there seemed to persist still the wind and violence of battle. We entered (I seem to recall) through the rear. Moon, trembling, his mouth parched, murmured that the events of the night were interesting; I dressed his wound and brought him a cup of tea; I was able to determine that his 'wound' was superficial. Suddenly he stammered in bewilderment, "You know, you ran a terrible risk." I told him not to worry about it. (The habit of the civil war had incited me to act as I did; besides, the capture of a single member could endanger our cause.) By the following day Moon had recovered his poise. He accepted a cigarette and subjected me to a severe interrogation on the "economic resources of our revolutionary party". His questions were very lucid; I told him (truthfully) that the situation was serious. Deep bursts of rifle fire agitated the south. I told Moon our comrades were waiting for us. My overcoat and my revolver were in my room; when I returned I found Moon straddled out on the sofa, his eyes closed. He imagined he had a fever; he invoked a painful spasm in his shoulder.

'At that moment I understood that his cowardice was irreparable. I clumsily entreated him to take care of himself and went out.

'Nine days we spent in the General's enormous house. Of the agonies and the successes of the war I shall not speak: I propose to relate the history of the scar that insults me. In my memory, those nine days form only a single day, save for the next to last, when our men broke into a barracks and we were able to avenge precisely the sixteen comrades who had been machine-gunned in Elphin. I slipped out of the house towards dawn, in the confusion of daybreak. At night-

fall I was back. My companion was waiting for me upstairs: his wound did not permit him to descend to the ground floor. I recall him having some volume of strategy in his hand, F. N. Maude or Clausewitz. "The
145 weapon I prefer is the artillery," he confessed to me one night. He inquired into our plans; he liked to censure them or revise them. He also was accustomed to denouncing our "deplorable economic basis"; dogmatic and gloomy, he predicted the disastrous end.
150 "C'est une affair flambée²," he murmured. In order to show that he was indifferent to being a physical coward, he magnified his mental arrogance. In this way, for good or bad, nine days elapsed.

'On the tenth day the city fell definitely to the Black
155 and Tans³. Tall silent horsemen patrolled the roads; ashes and smoke rode on the wind; on the corner I saw a corpse thrown to the ground, an impression less firm in my memory than that of a dummy on which the soldiers endlessly practised their markmanship, in the
160 middle of the square ... I had left when dawn was in the sky; before noon I returned. Moon, in the library, was speaking with someone; the tone of his voice told me he was talking on the telephone. Then I heard my name; then·that I would return at seven; then, the sug-
165 gestion that they should arrest me as I was crossing the garden. My reasonable friend was reasonably selling me out. I heard him demand guarantees of personal safety.

'Here my story becomes confused and lost. I know
170 that I pursued the informer along the black, night-marish halls and along deep stairways of dizziness. Moon knew the house very well, much better than I. One or two times I lost him. I cornered him before the soldiers stopped me. From one of the General's collec-
175 tion of arms I tore down a cutlass: with that half moon I carved into his face forever a half moon of blood. Borges, to you, a stranger, I have made this confession. Your contempt does not grieve me so much.'

Here the narrator stopped. I noticed that his hands
180 were shaking. 'And Moon?' I asked him.

'He collected his Judas money and fled to Brazil. That afternoon, in the square, he saw a dummy shot up by some drunken men.'

I waited in vain for the rest of the story. Finally I told
185 him to go on. Then a sob went through his body and with a weak gentleness he pointed to the whitish curved scar.

'You don't believe me?' he stammered. 'Don't you see that I carry written on my face the mark of infamy? I
190 have told you the story thus so that you would hear me to the end. I denounced the man who protected me; I am Vincent Moon. Now despise me.'

J. L. Borges

Notes
1 *apodictic* – pronouncing something in an unchallengeable way
2 *'C'est une affaire flambée'* – it's a burnt out cause.
3 *Black and Tans* – the police were reinforced by men from England, supposedly ex-officers who had served in the Great War. The new recruits, too numerous to be issued with regular uniforms, wore part dark police clothing and part khaki, hence the nickname 'Black and Tans'. Rumour had it that many had been recruited from English jails. They were highly paid and took full advantage of the power given to them.

THE SHAPE OF THE SWORD
SUMMARY

One of Moon's servants was eavesdropping and learned the truth about his master's background. He sells the story to a local newspaper. Write, in no more than 250 words, the newspaper article – *'The Englishman from La Colorada – True Story'* which reveals Moon's cowardly behaviour.

FOR DISCUSSION OR WRITING

1 What would your reaction be if you were the author and had just heard Moon's confession? Write a conclusion to the story showing your feelings.
2 Did you suspect at any stage that Moon and 'the Englishman from La Colorada' were one and the same?
3 What do you understand by the term 'cowardice'? What do you consider to be an act of cowardice?
4 Are there ever mitigating circumstances for cowardly behaviour?
5 Do you have a mental picture of a coward? Do you despise cowards?
6 Write about a situation in which you have or think you would experience cowardice within yourself?

THE HERO

'Jack fell as he'd have wished,' the Mother said,
And folded up the letter that she'd read.
'The Colonel writes so nicely.' Something broke
In the tired voice that quavered to a choke.
5 *She half looked up. 'We mothers are so proud*
Of our dead soldiers.' Then her face was bowed.

Quietly the Brother Officer went out.
He'd told the poor old dear some gallant lies
That she would nourish all her days no doubt.
10 *For while he coughed and mumbled, her weak eyes*
Had shone with gentle triumph, brimmed with joy,
Because he'd been so brave, her glorious boy.

He thought how 'Jack', cold-footed, useless swine,
15 *Had panicked down the trench that night the mine*
Went up at Wicked Corner; how he'd tried
To get sent home, and how, at last, he died,
Blown to small bits. And no one seemed to care
Except that lonely woman with white hair.

Siegfried Sassoon

THE HERO
FOR DISCUSSION OR WRITING

1 Do you feel pity for Jack?
2 Pretend you are Jack. Tell your story from the 'night the mine went up at Wicked Corner'.
3 Is the Brother Officer a coward because he does not tell Jack's mother the truth?
4 Can you describe an occasion when you thought that lying was justified?
5 What do you understand by the term 'a white lie'? Describe an occasion when you have told one.

THE HUMAN FACTOR

Maurice met and fell in love with Sarah when he was working in South Africa. She and her son, Sam, are black and to get them out of the country, to England, Maurice sought the help of Carson, a Communist friend.

Sarah came out to greet him as he was hanging his coat in the hall. She asked, 'Has something happened?'

'No.'

'You've never been as late as this without telephon-
10 ing.'

'Oh, I've been here and there, trying to see people. I couldn't find any of them in. I suppose they are all taking long weekends.'

'Will you have your whisky? Or do you want dinner
15 straight away?'

'Whisky. Make it a large one.'

'Larger than usual?'

'Yes, and no soda.'

'Something *has* happened.'

20 'Nothing important. But it's cold and wet almost like winter. Is Sam asleep?'

'Yes.'

'Where's Buller?'

'Looking for cats in the garden.'

25 He sat down in the usual chair and the usual silence fell between them. Normally he felt the silence like a comforting shawl thrown round his shoulders. Silence was relaxation, silence meant that words were unnecessary between the two of them – their love was too
30 established to need assurance; they had taken out a life policy in their love. But this night, with the original of Muller's notes in his pocket and his copy of it by this time in the hands of young Halliday, silence was like a vacuum in which he couldn't breathe: silence was a
35 lack of everything, even trust, it was a foretaste of the tomb.

'Another whisky, Sarah.'

'You *are* drinking too much. Remember poor Davis.'

'He didn't die of drink.'

40 'But I thought. . . .'

'You thought like all the others did. And you're wrong. If it's too much trouble to give me another whisky, say so and I'll help myself.'

'I only said remember Davis. . . .'

45 'I don't want to be looked after, Sarah. You are Sam's

---

mother, not mine.'

'Yes, I am his mother and you aren't even his father.'

They looked at each other in astonishment and dismay. Sarah said,

50 'I didn't mean....'

'It's not your fault.'

'I'm sorry.'

He said, 'This is what the future will be like if we can't talk. You asked me what I'd been doing. I've been 55 looking for someone to talk to all evening, but no one was there.'

'Talk about what?'

The question silenced him.

'Why can't you talk to *me*? Because *they* forbid it, I 60 suppose.

The Official Secrets Act – all that stupidity.'

'It's not them.'

'Then who?'

'When we came to England, Sarah, Carson sent 65 someone to see me. He had saved you and Sam. All he asked in return was a little help. I was grateful and I agreed.'

'What's wrong with that?'

'My mother told me when I was a child I always gave 70 away too much in a swap, but it wasn't too much for the man who saved you from BOSS. So there it is – I became what they call a double agent, Sarah. I rate a life-time in jail.'

Graham Greene

THE HUMAN FACTOR

FOR DISCUSSION OR WRITING

1 What does the word 'spy' mean to you?

2 Why do you think Graham Greene called his novel 'The Human Factor'? Does this throw any light on the character of a spy?

3 What punishment should a person receive if he is caught spying against his own country?

4 Write an essay entitled 'The Man who knew too Much'

COMPREHENSION

1 Why did Sarah ask Maurice, 'Has something happened?'? (2)

2 How does Maurice reply to Sarah's statement, 'Something *has* happened.'? (2)

3 In what ways does Maurice show that he is upset? (4)

4 What do you learn of the relationship between Maurice and Sarah? (4)

5 What is Maurice's official job? (1)

6 What has Maurice done to 'rate a life-time in jail'? What is the actual example that is causing him so much anxiety? (3)

7 What was Davis supposed to have died of? (1)

8 Who are 'they' on (line 59) (2)

9 What do the following phrases mean?
'They had taken out a life policy on their love' (line 30) (2)
'It was a foretaste of the tomb' (line 35) (2)
'I always gave away too much in a swap.' (line 69) (2)

MARLON BRANDO

Analyzing his rise and fall as a movie star, Brando told 'Oui' magazine: 'People pay money to have someone else act out their fantasies. It's like having a household pet: you endow the animal with qualities it 5 might not have. It is the same with an actor: you have one or two emotional experiences with him and you begin to trust him. He becomes your favourite fantasy-maker. But when his performances contradict your feelings or oppose your way of life, then it's a lousy 10 picture.'

It is an accurate interpretation of the star syndrome – up to a point – because in Hollywood every cloud must have a silver lining and every tragedy aspires to a happy ending. Through the ages, saints and heroes 15 went into the desert for meditation or around the world on perilous journeys or herculean tasks. In the twentieth century the stars, these last remants of ancient myths, are often forced into exile or plunged into decline until it is time for them to be newly acclaimed, 20 in the ritual known as 'the comeback'.

For an actor of Brando's dramatic stature and social influence nothing short of an apotheosis would do. And after nearly twenty years of disappointment and rejection he came back in 'The Godfather', a film safely on its way to being the highest grosser in box-office history. It reinstated Brando upon the throne he had all but abdicated. But restoration, as usual, was not easy; it involved the intrigues of partisans, the opposition of miscreants, the arbitrariness of timing, the fickleness of luck.

Mario Puzo claims a redoubtable casting coup when he insists he wrote 'The Godfather' with Brando in mind. It was a flash of author's intuition that failed to impress anyone else. When Paramount bought the novel, still in galley form, many names were initially shuffled for the part of Don Vito Corleone, including Anthony Quinn, Ernest Borgnine, Richard Conte, and even Carlo Ponti, Sophia Loren's producer husband. After Francis Ford Coppola was assigned to direct the film, he was intrigued by Puzo's original idea and called Brando. The actor desperately needed a popular success but was wary of yet another Mafia story, so soon after Kirk Douglas's 'The Brotherhood' had been indifferently received by critics and audiences.

Coppola insisted, and Brando who swore he had never read a novel in his whole life, looked over a first treatment of the screenplay and then dipped into the pages of the runaway best seller to get an impression of Don Corleone. He liked the role enough to submit to what to practically every other star would have been considered a crushing humiliation: he agreed to test for the part. The result is one of the most seductive legends in a legendary career. Brando himself conceived the rudimentary make-up; he plastered back his hair with grease, lined his cheeks and forehead with boot polish and stuffed Kleenex around his gums. Over a steaming cup of coffee he moved his prestidigitator's fingers and mumbled a few words.

Coppola brought the home-made test to the studio and ran it for a diffident high echelon. 'Sure he looks Italian,' they said defensively, 'but can he act?' When they learned it was actually Marlon Brando, a thrill of belated recognition electrified the meeting. Brando won the part but not the entire confidence of the studio. Too many flops weighed heavily on his star ledger; too many stories of past conflicts made him into a nearly unemployable sacred monster.

'The Godfather' was approached very tentatively as a film project. Coppola was given a very stringent, penny-pinching budget. Brando began the movie at his most cooperative, sinking himself into the part in Stanislavskian identification, treating his screen children – Al Pacino, James Caan, Robert Duvall – as if they were his own, developing a paternalistic, prankish attitude with them. Jokingly, Brando was

setting up the right atmosphere for an illusion of closely knit family life among the cast, but his lackadaisical behaviour frightened the front office. Brando could or would not remember his lines, which he read from notes written on his shirt cuffs, on cards behind the camera, or on strategically placed bits of paper strewn around the props. The alarm was sounded, and the old misconceptions bubbled up. 'Only Kazan can work with him,' was inevitably the first. There was talk of firing Coppola and hiring Kazan, but Brando steadfastly stood by the young man who had faith in him, threatening to quit if Coppola was ousted.

Both stayed, of course, after the Italian wedding sequence was shot and edited to perfect timing and dramatic cadence. The studio was pleased and the budget was considerably raised. 'The Godfather' looked good enough to venture a few more millions on. The caution now seems excessive and the sums parsimonious when compared with the goldmine the film became, with a gross of over 100 million dollars in its first year in general release.

Even before its premiere critics were gazing into their crystal balls to call it the 'Gone with the Wind' of gangster movies; but 'The Godfather' turned out to be not only a box-office explosion but also a very fine film. With a quality that goes beyond style into a cinematic alchemy, Coppola integrated the poetic vision of Visconti's 'Rocco and the Brothers' with the jazzy dynamism of 'Little Caesar'. The audience eavesdrops on these men who season their spaghetti between murders, who keep their women pure while prostituting others, and who split themselves right down the middle into private friends and public enemies.

Everything in the film falls into place with a smooth precision that is never mechanical: the casting is inspired, the period recreation flawless, Coppola's control of the disparate elements unflagging. But 'The Godfather' needs a godlike figure at its core. Brando gives it emotional roots: the good-bad, two-faced Janus of the early films now wears a cragged, eroded mask, but the everlasting ambivalence lurks in every wrinkle.

Brando's performance is a wonder of observation and understatement. He had the Italian accent and gesture down pat: the defiant-apologetic shrug, the hands that helplessly shoot up, the evanescent whiff of an 'a' at the end of each noun. Yet he is neither Vittorio de Sica nor Henry Armetta, for he found the essence at the bottom of the heady caricature. His cracked, dim voice suggests untold maladies, deeply inhaled Sicilian cigarettes, or the whirr of crushed coffee beans in an espresso machine. All the minute touches dovetail into the portrait of an aging monster, a tyrant grown benign.

René Jordan

MARLON BRANDO
MULTIPLE CHOICE

1 Brando says that you like
certain actors because:
A they are emotional
B they are reliable
C they represent your hidden
feelings
D they are like your pets

2 The nearest word in meaning
to 'herculean' (line 16) is:
A difficult
B lonely
C thoughtful
D long lasting

3 Modern film stars are like
ancient heroes because:
A they go to the desert
B they disappear from public
view and later return in
triumph
C they meditate
D they travel a great deal

4 Another phrase or word for
'apotheosis' (line 22) is:
A made to reappear like a
god
B rejection
C highly profitable
D dramatic

5 The author of 'The Godfather'
chose Brando:
A by casting his mind back
B after a sudden insight
C after shuffling several
names
D after failing to impress
anyone

6 Brando hesitated before
accepting the role because:
A he was desperate for a part
B a similar theme had not
been popular
C he had already been in a
film about the Mafia
D this film was different

7 The selection committee were
doubtful of Brando because of
ONE of the following:
A he had been unemployed
B he mumbled
C they took a long time to
recognise him
D he had been difficult to
work with in the past

8 'Tentatively' (line 69) means:
A economically
B hesitantly
C fearfully
D trying

9 The author mentions all the
following problems except
ONE:
A Brando was too casual
B Brando only acted well with
one director
C People mistrusted Brando's
ability
D Brando did not get on well
with the other actors

10 All except ONE of the
following were signs that the
production was going well:
A scenes of a festivity
excellently executed
B everyone became more
cautious
C more financial help was
forthcoming
D director and principal actor
agreed to continue

11 The film has the following
qualities except ONE
A poetry
B liveliness
C intimacy
D mechanical rhythm

12 The word 'disparate' (line 113)
is closest in meaning to:
A without hope
B different
C separated
D awkward

13 Brando depicts Don Corleone
by all except ONE of these
means:
A pronunciation
B mannerisms
C restraint
D helplessness

14 The word nearest in meaning
to 'benign' (line 128) is:
A powerful
B gentle
C old
D weak

VISITING THE DEAD

When she was found
Her tongue protruded from her gums;
Her face was knuckled,
Her hand clenched on her sheet.

5 Now her skin has eased out,
New-washed cloth in which the wrinkles fade
Beneath the iron's hiss.
They have lain her out in clean linen.

We drink tea from her best china.
10 A knot of mourners unravels upstairs;
A maiden aunt descends, weeping softly
Into her starched handkerchief.

When they brought down the body,
The coffin stuck in the crooked staircase,
15 We hesitated, awkward in our best suits,
Then we rushed to help and freed her.

Ciarán Carson

VISITING THE DEAD
FOR DISCUSSION OR WRITING

1 Did you find the poem upsetting? If so, why?
2 The Poet experienced a moment of embarrassment when the coffin got stuck on the staircase. Have you ever found yourself in an awkward situation when you could not find the right words to say or the right action to make? Write about this.

THE MAYOR OF CASTERBRIDGE

Susan, the mayor's wife has died and is survived by her daughter, Elizabeth-Jane. The locals are discussing her death:

At the town-pump there were gathered (when he
5 passed) a few old inhabitants, who came there for water whenever they had, as at present, spare time to fetch it, because it was purer from that original fount than from their own wells. Mrs. Cuxsom, who had been there for an indefinite time with her pitcher, was
10 describing the incidents of Mrs. Henchard's death, as she had learnt them from the nurse.

'And she was as white as marble-stone,' said Mrs. Cuxsom. 'And like-wise such a thoughtful woman, too – ah, poor soul – that 'a minded every little thing that
15 wanted tending. "Yes," says she, "when I'm gone, and my last breath's blowed, look in the top drawer o' the chest in the back room by the window, and you'll find all my coffin clothes; a piece of flannel – that's to put under me, and the little piece is to put under my head;
20 and my new stockings for my feet – they are folded alongside, and all my other things. And there's four ounce pennies, the heaviest I could find, a-tied up in bits of linen, for weights – two for my right eye and two for my left," she said. "And when you've used 'em, and
25 my eyes don't open no more, bury the pennies, good souls, and don't ye go spending 'em, for I shouldn't like

it. And open the windows as soon as I am carried out, and make it as cheerful as you can for Elizabeth-Jane."'

'Ah, poor heart!'

30 'Well, and Martha did it, and buried the ounce pennies in the garden. But if ye'll believe words, that man, Christopher Coney, went and dug 'em up, and spent 'em at The Three Mariners. "Faith," he said, "why should death rob life o' fourpence? Death's not of such
35 good report that we should respect 'en to that extent," says he.'

''Twas a cannibal deed!' deprecated her listeners.

'Gad, then, I won't quite ha'e it,' said Solomon Longways. 'I say it today, and 'tis a Sunday morning, and
40 I wouldn't speak wrongfully for a zilver zixpence at such a time. I don't see noo harm in it. To respect the dead is sound doxology; and I wouldn't sell skellintons – leastwise respectable skellintons – to be varnished for 'natomies, except I were out o' work. But money is
45 scarce, and throats get dry. Why *should* death rob life o' fourpence? I say there was no treason in it.'

'Well, poor soul; she's helpless to hinder that or anything now,' answered Mother Cuxsom. 'And all her shining keys will be took from her, and her cupboards
50 opened; and little things 'a didn't wish seen, anybody will see; and her wishes and ways will all be as nothing!'

Thomas Hardy

THE MAYOR OF CASTERBRIDGE
FOR DISCUSSION OR WRITING

1 Do you agree that what Christopher Coney did was 'a cannibal deed' or would you accept and sympathise with Solomon Longways when he defends the action thus: 'But money is scarce, and throats get dry. Why *should* death rob life o' fourpence? I say there was no treason in it.'?

2 In your experience, how true is the old saying 'Out of sight, out of mind'?

3 Think of someone well-known or close to you who has died. Describe two or three things about the person you remember most vividly.

GROWING UP

GROWING UP

PRAYER BEFORE BIRTH

Let me, the womb dweller, live to see birth.

May my cell of sustenance deliver me unscathed
Into the breathless, rushing trauma of life.
May I not starve in the ghettos of humanity;
5 Nor live bloated on the fat of the poor.

As I am so safely suspended here,
May I be in the life after life.
May my time on earth be peaceful;
Not harassed by the tormented fantasies of idiots and
10   fools.

Let me pass into old age with dignity.
May I not be impaired in vision or sense
Or troubled by collapse of health, so that
I may pass out of this life as I came in:
15   With Hope.

Jacquelyn Barker (14)

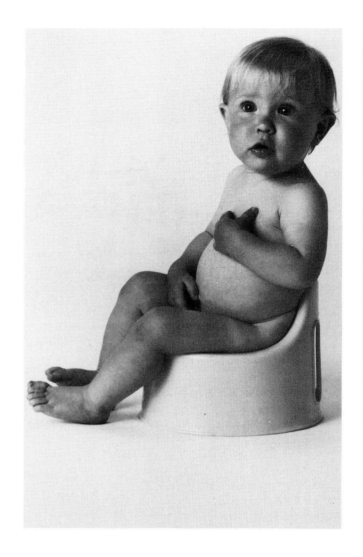

PRAYER BEFORE BIRTH
FOR DISCUSSION OR WRITING

1 Is is difficult to maintain one's individuality in modern society? Are we programmed from the moment of birth?
2 What would your wishes be for your child? Write a poem 'A Prayer for my son/daughter'.
3 The birth of a healthy baby is surely one of the happiest moments in a couple's experience. Give an account of the happiest moment in your life.

THE ALMOND TREE
(adapted from)

I
All the way to the hospital
the lights were green as peppermints.
Trees of black iron broke into leaf
ahead of me, as if
5 I were the lucky prince
in an enchanted wood
summoning summer with my whistle,
banishing winter with a nod.

Swung by the road from bend to bend,
10 I was aware that blood was running
down through the delta of my wrist
and under arches
of bright bone. Centuries,
continents it had crossed;
15 from an undisclosed beginning
spiralling to an unmapped end.

II
Crossing (at sixty) Magdalen Bridge
Let it be a son, a son, said
the man in the driving mirror,
20 *Let it be a son. The tower*
held up its hand: the college
bells shook their blessing on his head.

III
I parked in an almond's
shadow blossom, for the tree
25 *was waving, waving me*
upstairs with a child's hands.

IV
Up
the spinal stair
and at the top
30 *along*
a bone-white corridor
the blood tide swung
me swung me to a room
whose walls shuddered
35 *with the shuddering womb.*
Under the sheet
wave after wave, wave
after wave beat
on the bone coast, bringing
40 *ashore – whom?*
                    New –
minted, my bright farthing!
Coined by our love, stamped with
our images, how you
45 *enrich us! Both*
you make one. Welcome
to your white sheet,
my best poem!

V
At seven-thirty
50 *the visitors' bell*
scissored the calm
of the corridors.
The doctor walked with me
to the slicing doors.
55 *His hand upon my arm,*
his voice – I have to tell
you – set another bell
beating in my head:
your son is a mongol
60 *the doctor said.*

VI
How easily the word went in –
clean as a bullet
leaving no mark on the skin,
stopping the heart within it.

65 *This was my first death.*
The 'I' ascending on a slow
last thermal breath
studied the man below
as a pilot treading air might
70 *the buckled shell of his plane –*
boot, glove, and helmet
feeling no pain

from the snapped wires' radiant ends.
Looking down from a thousand feet
75 *I held four walls in the lens*
of an eye; wall, window, the street
a torrent of windscreens, my own
car under its almond tree,
and the almond waving me down.
80 *I wrestled against gravity,*

but light was melting and the gulf
cracked open. Unfamiliar
the body of my late self
I carried to the car.

VIII
85 *You turn to the window for the first time.*
I am called to the cot
to see your focus shift.
Take tendril-hold on a shaft
of sun, explore its dusty surface, climb
90 *to an eye you cannot*
meet. You have a sickness they cannot heal
the doctors say: locked in
your body you will remain.
Well, I have been locked in mine.
95 *We will tunnel each other out. You seal*
the covenant with a grin.

In the days we have known one another,
my little mongol love,
I have learnt more from your lips
100 *than you will from mine perhaps:*
I have learnt that to live is to suffer,
to suffer is to live.
                    Jon Stallworthy

THERE IS NO SUCH THING
AS A SHARK

Once upon a time there lived in Moscow a pedologist[1] by the name of Stanchinskaia and a very strange thing happened to this pedologist.

She was also a mother and did everything in her power to protect her son from fairy tales. Even when she talked to him about animals she made sure to mention only those he had seen with his own eyes. After all he had to grow up a realist! The fewer harmful fantasies the better! She considered especially harmful fairy tales that told about supernatural transformations – werewolves, Baba-Yagas, and others.

This ardent foe of the fairy tale even published an article in a Moscow magazine in which she wrote:

'We propose to replace the unrealistic folk tales and fantasies with simple, realistic stories taken from the world of reality and from nature.'

No compromises, no weakening! Let us get rid of all fairy tales, epic tales, the entire folklore of Russia and of the rest of the world – without any exception. And everything would have been just fine, but, unfortunately, as a loving mother, she began to keep a most detailed diary about her little son. Without being aware of it, she contradicted, in her entries, all her favourite arguments about the harmful influences of fantastic tales and destroyed with her own pen, so to speak, her formidable theories.

She wrote in this diary – and it has been published – that her boy, as if to make up for the fairy tales of which he had been deprived, began to spin from morning till night the wildest fantasies. He pretended that a red elephant came to live in his room; he invented a friend – a bear whom he names Cora; and he would often say, 'Please, don't sit on the chair next to mine because – can't you see? – the she-bear is sitting on it.' And

'Mother, why are you walking right on top of the wolves? Can't you see the wolves standing there?'

And with the first snow he became a reindeer, a little reindeer in a Siberian forest. And if he sat on a rug, the rug would immediately be transformed into a ship. At any time with the power of his childish fantasy, he could draw any animal out of the air. His mother wrote in the diary:

'Today he returned home carrying something very carefully:

"Mommie, I brought you a little tiger," and he extended to me his empty hand.

"Do you like my baby tiger?"

"Yes, yes my little one!"

"Let him stay with us," he pleaded. Before sitting down to dinner he placed next to his plate a smaller one, and when his food was brought to him, he said:

"And for the baby tiger?"

Once he recounted in a lively manner: "I went down to the sea and splashed about for a while. Then, suddenly, a big tiger came. I hid myself under the shore then I threw out a net and caught a fish."

"Where is the fish?"

"I ate it up – raw!"

Most of his days were spent this way. Every minute he made up some fairy tale for himself: "Mother, a bug came to visit me. He wanted to shake hands with me and put out his little paw...".'

And although his mother observed that he literally bathed in fantasies as in a river, she continued to 'protect' him from the ill effects of books of fairy tales.

As if there were a basic difference between the fairy

tale that a child made up for himself and one that was created for him (as a folk tale) by imaginative folk or by a good writer. It makes no difference whether or not the child is offered fairy tales for, if he is not, he becomes his own Anderson, Grimm, Ershov. Moreover all his playing is a dramatization of a fairy tale which he creates on the spot, animating, according to his fancy, all objects – converting any stool into a train, into a house, into an aeroplane, or into a camel.

Kornei Chukovsky.

Notes
1 Pedologist – someone who studies the nature of children

HELLO, HELLO – SPEAK UP TIGER!

Katie is just three. She telephones her tiger at least five times a day, to tell him the latest news – what Mummy is up to, why brother William is being so beastly, and so on. Tiger doesn't exist but he is a greedy animal and always turns up for meals – he even has his own chair. He pays for this hospitality, though; whenever things around the house get broken his job is to get the blame.

Some parents are greatly disturbed by the imaginary Teddies, 'Milk Shakes', sisters who aren't there, tigers that don't snarl, and invisible rabbits that sit under the dining table. As the famous child psychologist, Bruno Bettenheim, has said: 'An imaginary companion is a symptom and the question to be answered is: "Of what is it a symptom?".'

However, a new study, of 141 three and four year olds, suggests that there is absolutely no need for parents to worry when their children suddenly develop invisible and imaginary 'friends'. And that, in fact, children who have them are in almost every respect better off than those without.

For instance, the study, carried out by Dr. Jerome Singer at Yale, found that as many as 65 per cent of three and four year olds admit to having imaginary friends – so if some sort of worry is what causes these friends, the worries are pretty common. But this 65 per cent with invisible friends does differ sharply from other children.

The study showed them to be less aggressive, more co-operative. Dr. Singer found that for some reason they smile more, show a greater ability to concentrate and their language is considerably more advanced.

Perhaps most encouraging of all, the children with imaginary companions watch less television – only half as much in fact. Even when they do watch the box their choice of programmes is apparently quite different – they are less interested in the cartoons and violent programmes that other children prefer.

All in all, it seems that it is the brighter child who develops imaginary playmates. They are more likely to be firstborn or to have no brothers or sisters (due to an early death, for example). But there is little evidence in the study to suggest that the children are in any way pre-occupied with particularly serious worries which causes the arrival of these friends.

In fact, Dr. Singer says, 'Imaginary companions can be seen as a sign of health. These children are able to make their own world. Yet they have a strong sense of what's real and what's fantasy... When you question them about one of their imaginary playmates, they may say, "That's just make-believe".'

It is transitional worries that seem to be the cause of many imaginary companions – and they fade away as the worry itself passes. One two-year-old girl, for instance, developed a friend which she called the 'Laughing Tiger' who arrived at the time when the girl was very frightened of the animals in her neighbourhood, dogs especially, which could bite. It seems as if this girl faced her fear of the dogs by inventing her own ferocious animal that wasn't ferocious at all. He didn't roar, never scared children, didn't bite – just laughed. When 'Laughing Tiger' finally faded away several months after his arrival, the young girl's fear of dogs had vanished as well.

In another case, three children were separated from their mother, who went into hospital, and lived with their (extremely ancient) grandmother. Two of the children developed all kinds of difficulties – they wet the bed, couldn't sleep, had difficulties making new friends. But the third child, Miriam, withdrew into a world of her own, inhabited only by herself and 'Susan', an imaginary friend. Susan apparently became Miriam's 'daughter', thus mirroring to some degree the relationship Miriam had recently lost. The new relationship continued until Miriam did make a close friend at school.

Imaginary friends are most prevalent, it appears, around the ages of three and four, when they are usually animals or TV characters (most often of indeterminate sex) and then again around nine and ten, when male friends seem to be preferred. It is only if they occur at other ages, especially if four year olds carry their friends with them to school at five or six, that invisible companions should be regarded as more serious 85 problems.

But in general the picture is encouraging. As one psychiatrist who has studied imaginary children in Chicago and London, sums up: 'Only children who are gifted produce imaginary companions. You never see 90 them with a dumb child.'

Arnold Legh
SUNDAY TIMES

HELLO, HELLO – SPEAK UP TIGER
SUMMARY

A friend is worried about his/her child who has suddenly 'acquired' an imaginary friend. In no more than 200 words summarise the information given in 'Hello, Hello – speak up Tiger' which offers comfort to such parents.

THERE IS NO SUCH THING AS A SHARK
HELLO, HELLO-SPEAK UP TIGER
FOR DISCUSSION OR WRITING

1 The pedologist was determined her son should 'grow up a realist'. Why do you think she felt this was important?

2 Did you have an imaginary companion when you were young? What was the fantasy world you both inhabited?

3 Do your brothers, sisters or young relatives have an imaginary playmate? What have they told you about 'it'?

4 Did violent programmes or horror films on television frighten you when you were young? Can you remember any such programmes and the feelings they evoked in you?

5 Should parents decide what their children read and view? If you think that they should, what types of reading material, television programmes and films do you feel need attention?

6 Is Public Censorship necessary? Write an essay giving points for and points against censorship, ending with your personal viewpoint.

THE LITTLE GIRL AND THE WOLF

One afternoon a big wolf waited in a dark forest for a little girl to come along carrying a basket of food to her grandmother. Finally a little girl did come along and she was carrying a basket of food. 'Are you carrying
5 that basket of food to your grandmother?' asked the wolf. The little girl said yes, she was. So the wolf asked her where her grandmother lived and the little girl told him, and he disappeared into the wood.

When the little girl opened the door of her grand-
10 mother's house she saw that there was somebody in bed with a nightcap and nightgown on. She approached nearer, then twenty-five feet from the bed she saw that it was not her grandmother but the wolf, for even in a nightgown a wolf does not look any more
15 like your grandmother than the Metro-Goldwyn lion looks like Calvin Coolidge. So the little girl took an automatic out of her basket and shot the wolf dead.
MORAL: It is not so easy to fool little girls nowadays as it used to be.

James Thurber

> **THE LITTLE GIRL AND THE WOLF**
> **FOR DISCUSSION OR WRITING**
>
> **1** Choose your favourite fairystory and rewrite it. Use the basic plot but have a subtle twist to the traditional story. Include, at the end, a moral.

BYE-CHILD

He was discovered in a henhouse where she had confined him.
He was incapable of saying anything.

When the lamp glowed,
5 *A yolk of light*
In their back window,
The child in the outhouse
Put his eye to the chink –

Little henhouse boy,
10 *Sharp-faced as new moons*
Remembered, your photo still
Glimpsed like a rodent
On the floor of my mind,

Little moon man,
15 *Kennelled and faithful*
At the foot of the yard,
Your frail shape, luminous,
Weightless, is stirring the dust,

The cobwebs, old droppings
20 *Under the roosts*
And dry smells from scraps
She put through your trapdoor
Morning and evening.

After those footsteps, silence;
25 *Vigils, solitudes, fasts,*
Unchristened tears,
A puzzled love of the light.
But now you speak at last

With a remote mime
30 *Of something beyond patience,*
Your gaping wordless proof
Of lunar distances
Travelled beyond love.

Seamus Heaney

PATRICK

Take the case of Patrick whose mother was unable to face the scorn of her community when she had an illegitimate child. The whole thing came to light because of a small boy's love of fishing. Sitting by a
5 river catching tiddlers Thomas heard strange sounds coming from a nearby chicken house, chicken noises, and yet they seemed unlike any chicken talk he'd heard before. When he mentioned this at home his father told him not to be stupid. Thomas was not put off.
10 The next time he went fishing he went up to the hut and found that the sacking which covered its windows ended an inch from the sill, leaving an air vent. A

The faces change.
The bruises don't.

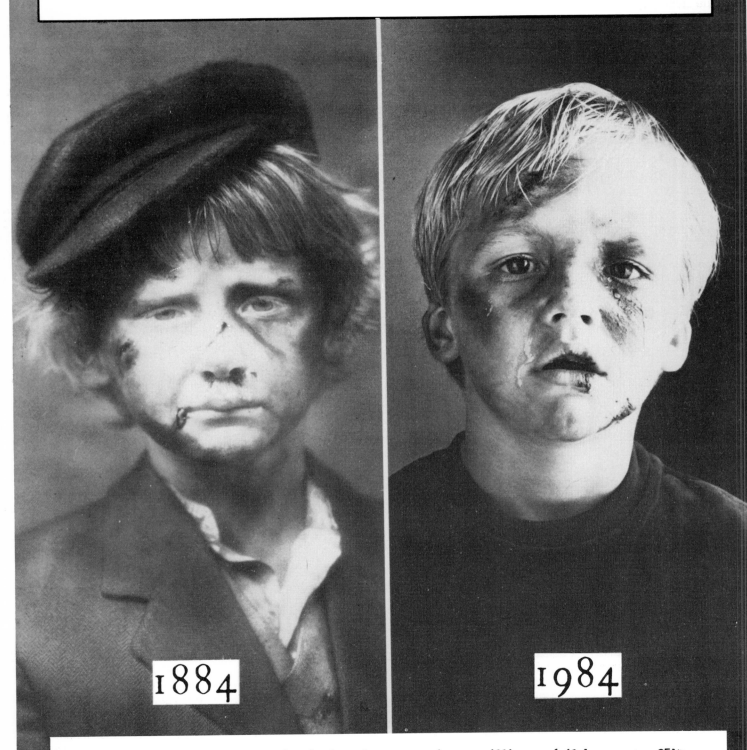

1884

1984

finger poked through and Thomas put his own hand over it, almost like a sign of friendship. He ran home.

15 His father still refused to believe him, finding it quite an incredible story since the field belonged to one of the most respected women in the village, a widow with four grown children. But Thomas wouldn't give up and the next day he managed to pull away the sacking.

20 What looked back at him was recognisably the face of a child, but it was so horrifying with its ingrained dirt, waist-length matted hair and strange chicken-like talk, that Thomas was terrified. He ran home and his father did believe him.

25 When Patrick was finally discovered he was seven and a half years old. His parents were intelligent and he appeared to be a normal healthy baby when he left the Nursing Home where he was born. He was fostered at once, the putative father paying the foster

30 mother. But, two years later, the payments stopped and he was returned to his mother who hid him in the chicken house. This was ten foot by six foot and fitted with wire racks from which the wire had been removed leaving Patrick to perch on wooden struts.

35 He moved along these bars in a sort of see-saw movement and hopped about in frog-like movements from the back of his legs to his forearms. His toenails were so long that he constantly tripped over them and 28 healed fractures were found in his legs and arms

40 from his falls. Having lived so long in the dark his face was deathly pale, and his shin bones were concave, presumably in part because of his diet which consisted of crusts and potato peelings thrown to him as it might be to pigs. The floor of the hut was blanketed with

45 layers of chicken feathers, excreta and the remains of food.

Surgery has now straightened his legs and he is now able to walk, although with a slightly rolling gait. It seems unlikely that he will ever learn to talk since he

50 was beyond learning when rescued, and until then he had heard only the hens in the neighbouring hut and imitated them. His mother received a sentence of nine months' imprisonment.

PATRICK AND BYE-CHILD
FOR DISCUSSION OR WRITING

1 Which piece of writing did you feel was the more successful in conveying the child's horrendous existence? Give reasons for your answer.
2 Is having an illegitimate child still a social tabu in our society?
3 In the prose passage the narrator remains neutral but Seamus Heaney includes his personal feelings in the poem. How does each writer's technique influence your reaction to the incident described?
4 Do you think the punishment the mother received was fair?
5 Write the mother's statement to the court in her own defence.

ORDINARY FAMILIES
(adapted from)

Margaret and I quarrelled because she would not let me sink her makeshift boat in the marsh pool, in which a fine steep sea could be worked up by hand in a few seconds. More exactly, I quarrelled with Margaret

5 about it, for my sister always remained passive in the many disagreements we had when I was getting on for eleven and she was nine.

I loved wrecks when the boats were only old cardboard picnic plates, like these. The whole family was

10 taken sailing by father so often, in such filthy weather, that I found much delight in watching an unseaworthy craft get a bucketing and eventually founder when there was no personal anxiety attached to the performance.

15 But Margaret was naturally more of a sailor than I was: she had my father's liking for unsound craft. Her boat must stay afloat as long as possible.

I pressed my suggestion, pointing out that we could not spend all day messing about with a rotten old plate.

20 Margaret went on playing with her greasy plate, and I might not have been there, for all the notice she took.

In her place Ronald, my brother, or my other sister, Dru, who were both out sailing with father, would have argued hotly that having sunk my own plate I had no

The details are beyond recall, but the main theme on which I harped was that she had been taken out of an orphan home for me to play with. Had she never thought it funny that she should be dark when the rest of us were not? The pleasing arrogance of the notion was wasted on her. I followed it up by saying carelessly that I had only to say the word at home and she would go back. She began to gulp. To both of us that mysterious thing, an orphan home, was a place of unimaginable horror.

right to wreck theirs, but Margaret went on her own way imperturbably as usual, and, as usual, this exasperated me.

I insisted that she should let me have the plate to sink, adding that 'She'd better,' because the repetition of the order was having no effect.

Margaret lifted wonderful dark eyes to me indifferently, and asked why.

'Because you just had!' was the inevitable answer to that question in our family. This gave the threatener a second or two in which to cast about in his or her mind for a reason.

'Why, Lallie? Why'd I better?'

I said, on the inspiration of the moment, that I must not tell her that.

A light breeze of fancy was stirring in my mind: would it hold and freshen, or die away? – Well, if I did tell her, would she keep a secret?

She promised. I told her that she was not really my sister; she did not belong to us at all. I was amazed at the unaccustomed speed with which my thoughts were gathering way and fairly scudding along before the breeze of fancy. It was strengthening nicely.

'Lallie!'

What else was I going to tell her? I should have preferred more time in which to think this out. But at least she was properly conscious of my existence now. I see her, either as she was or as my imagination afterwards painted her, staring across the narrow pool at me, one hand fingering her mouth apprehensively: there must have been something triumphantly ominous in my tone, even though I was uncertain what was to come next. Vague resentment against Margaret, who secured all the attention that I coveted, may have sharpened my powers of invention, but mainly I think I was carried away by the conscienceless joy of creation as bit by bit I adopted circumstantial evidence into the story I was evolving.

The two older ones, Ronald and Dru, had each other for company, I pointed out, and she knew that the baby between me and Ronald had died. So naturally my parents felt I ought to have someone too. But not if I preferred it otherwise. (If only that were true! I thought.)

In order to prolong this savoury moment to the utmost I loaded it with as much repetition as Margaret would stand. Credulity grew in me as it did in her while I added subsidiary details. One of them, of which I was proud enough for it to stick in my mind, was that I myself had picked her out from the other babies in the home and begged my kindly parents to let me keep this one as against a rival choice of their own: a good touch that. I saw the orphan home; a long and dismal row of iron beds, like those in the Ipswich hospital where my tonsils had been removed. The wind of imagination was blowing great guns by this time, and it was the frail barque of fair play (so deeply venerated in the Rush family) that was properly pooped and sunk, leaving the sodden plate still floating almost forgotten on the pool. In decency Margaret ought to do every-

and the orphan homes in my prayers. We were allowed to say these kneeling humped up between the sheets in cold weather. But I was always chary of ¹³⁰ drawing the Lord's attention to small lapses from grace which, but for my stressing, He might have been willing to overlook.

E. Arnot Robertson

⁹⁵ thing I wanted, I gave her to understand, because if I had not chosen her, where would she be now? And who? Certainly not a Rush!

I gave this time to sink in.

'Now you let me have the plate!' I said, and the ¹⁰⁰ moment stands out sweetly in memory. 'Shove her right over. There! Look! Look, Margaret, she's going.' But Margaret was crying too hard to watch the jolly swamping. The noise she made did not matter: mother never came down to the water in the mornings and the ¹⁰⁵ rest of the family was almost out of sight down the estuary. There was even an advantage in her weeping: it left her in no condition to question my next statement, for which I could think of no support. If they discovered at home that she knew about this, they would send her ¹¹⁰ back at once; she had better not let them guess!

The unhappy child nodded and made an effort at self-control, but it was not successful for some time. I was afraid that she would not cheer up in time for lunch, but fear helped her here.

¹¹⁵ In the evening I began to feel slightly guilty about my invention after mother had said good night. Remorse, I had discovered, was in some way related to the prone position, because I was only sorry about things when I was in bed, and when, for a week or so ¹²⁰ after I came home without my tonsils, they made me lie down in a darkened room in the afternoons, I found my conscience pricked by numbers of things which would not have otherwise stayed in my mind until night and repentance overtook me. So for a while I sat up in bed ¹²⁵ in order to keep an unbiased view while I worried as to whether I had better mention this matter of Margaret

A PORTRAIT OF THE ARTIST AS A YOUNG MAN

'I am Stephen Dedalus. I am walking beside my father whose name is Simon Dedalus. We are in Cork, in Ireland. Cork is a city. Our room is in the Victoria Hotel. Victoria and Stephen and Simon. Simon and
5 Stephen and Victoria. Names.

The memory of his childhood suddenly grew dim. He tried to call forth some of its vivid moments but could not. He recalled only names. Dante, Parnell, Clare, Clongowes. A little boy had been taught geogra-
10 phy by an old woman who kept two brushes in her wardrobe. Then he had been sent away from home to a college, he had made his first communion and eaten slim jim out of his cricket cap and watched the firelight leaping and dancing on the wall of a little bedroom in
15 the infirmary and dreamed of being dead, of mass being said for him by the rector in a black and gold cope, of being buried then in the little graveyard of the community off the main avenue of limes. But he had not died then. Parnell had died. There had been no mass
20 for the dead in the chapel and no procession. He had not died but he had faded out like a film in the sun. He had been lost or had wandered out of existence for he no longer existed. How strange to think of him passing out of existence in such a way, not by death but by
25 fading out in the sun or by being lost and forgotten somewhere in the universe! It was strange to see his small body appear again for a moment: a little boy in a grey belted suit. His hands were in his side pockets and his trousers were tucked in at the knees by elastic
30 bands.'

James Joyce

---

*A PORTRAIT OF THE ARTIST AS A
YOUNG MAN*
FOR DISCUSSION OR WRITING

1 What are your memories of childhood? Is it a period you are glad to have left or would you like to relive it? Give a reason for your answer.
2 Look at photographs of yourself as a child and more recent ones. Do you feel yourself distanced, in the way Stephen does, from your former self?
3 Describe your favourite childhood memory or an incident you remember vividly.
4 Do you like your forename? If you could have chosen your own name what would it have been? Why?
5 What name would you hate to have been called? Why?

MECHANICS

My father worked above me, a spanner in his hand.
In the lemon sunlight he was a shadow against the blue
  sky;
A delicate blue, almost watery in the heat.
5 Beyond him yawned a sleepy field of green and
  yellow;
Cowslips nestled in the long grass like drops of honey.

But I became oblivious to the call of the summer landscape.
10 The gravel clawed at my bare legs as I sat beneath my
  father,
He dripped oil on my naked hot hands
And ruffled my hair with grimy, thick fingers.

The sun curved down to the hazy horizon
15 And the odour of searing rubber and sweating grease
Mingled with the soft flowery fragrance of evening.
A breeze delivered each smell to probe my nostrils
And my father rubbed my hands clean with a filthy rag.
Diane Burgess (15)

'Mechanics' is part of a childhood memory. During one of a series of poetry workshops with the poet Alan Brownjohn, we were asked to think of a colour, smell, taste or sound which brings to mind a vivid image and use it to recall the past. This was a completely new way of writing poetry to me and certainly proved effective. It is a method I still use now and I find it can usually remain undetected in the finished poem. No one would have thought that the inspiration for 'Mechanics' was the colour green. At certain times a bright green reminds me of the 'Swarfega' which my father often used to clean my hands when I had been playing. The poem is an extension of this simple memory: my father used to maintain his cousin's Go-Kart at race-meetings and although the track was surrounded by attractive meadows I was always drawn to the filth and noise of the machinery.

Diane Burgess

OUR YOUTH NOW LOVE LUXURY

Our youth now love luxury
They have bad manners,
Contempt for antiquity,
Disrespect for older people.
5 *Children nowadays are tyrants.*
They no longer rise when their elders
Enter the room.
They contradict their parents,
Chatter before company,
10 *Gobble their food,*
And tyrannise their teachers.

Plato
Fourth Century B.C.

Cambridge[1] isn't very far from Newton in space, but miles away in culture, and my children had their first taste of culture shock. Newton is a nice suburb town with good schools and privileged youngsters and con-siderable social order of the white respectable variety. Cambridge is racially and economically mixed. Around Harvard and MIT[2] there are well-to-do young-sters buying an apple for a quarter at Nini's, eating at ethnic restaurants, shopping at the expensive clothes stores around Holyoke Center. Where we lived it was blue-collar, Irish, Italian, and some blacks, largely Catholic, and very rough. I hadn't been worried about this at all because the same thing happened to me when my mother left my father. We had been living in the suburbs, but we moved to a rough neighbourhood near Boston after the divorce. And I'd loved that neigh-bourhood, it had seemed alive to me, and I'd learned a lot from living there. I just assumed things would be the same for my kids.

And maybe they would have been, except for the time – it was the late Sixties when we moved, 1968 to be exact. The school was torn by racial strife, late-sixties rhetoric, even bomb scares. And riddled with drugs of all sorts. The bigotry of the school adminis-tration served to legitimate attacks on blacks by white kids, and it was difficult not to take sides. Within a week of starting school, Elspeth had changed. She'd given up the good girl, she found a group of friends, she was out all the time. Within a month, she was a dif-ferent person, and I no longer knew her.

She fell in with a group of youngsters I liked very much – they were racially mixed, smart, and had a kind of gentleness in their hearts. But they were also unhappy and protesting and used drugs. And their protest took other forms – they skipped school, they shoplifted, they did dope and uppers and all the rest.

Elspeth's closest friend was a girl named Selene, a gorgeous girl with Asiatic blood who had been to school in Switzerland and England, had moved around the world with her professor father. She was very intel-ligent but extremely wary of adults. She looked at me always as if she were listening not to what I was saying but to what posture I was taking, as if she were prepar-ing a posture that could encompass mine, could manipulate it. But I was never saying anything import-ant to her, just asking about school or the movie or whatever they'd been doing. But I think she thought I was always checking up on where they'd been.

Because there was some reason to. Elspeth had stopped, completely, helping around the house. She refused even to clean her room, and one weekend when I couldn't stand it any more, I went in to clean it myself. And I found ... things. Stuffed under the bed, in the back of her closet, stuck in bureau drawers: things she couldn't use, and couldn't afford. Tens of packages of pantihose, packaged bras in sizes she couldn't wear, lipsticks, blushers, mascara still in the plastic wrap, and magazines, tens of them, the glossy ones like Vogue that Els couldn't afford on her two-dollar allow-ance. Except for the magazines, only a package of pantihose had been opened. Opened, and the hose stuffed back in the wrapping, because they were extra-longs, a size Els couldn't use.

I talked to Elspeth, of course. She didn't deny the shoplifting, but she would not promise to stop. She shrugged when I told her the trouble she could get into. It was fun, she said, and Selene had been doing it for years and had never been caught. You would not get caught if you were clever, she said.

It was obvious she wasn't stealing things to use them, in fact her appropriation of the unusable seemed almost intentional. That way, perhaps she worked it out, she wasn't *stealing*, but going through a puberty rite that involved danger and risk. She listened to me wide-eyed when I warned her about it, but her face didn't change. She was beginning to be as bland-faced as Selene.

Also, she was doing poorly in school. Els had an IQ of 150. There was no reason for her to be failing, but she was. Her highest grade was in the seventies on her end-of-term report, and some were in the thirties and forties. Again, we had a talk. Again, I encountered no opposition, but no acceptance. I told her she would some day want to go to college, would want to go to a good college, but would not be able to get in because of what she was doing now. She looked at me.

In the spring, she was expelled from school, but didn't tell me about it for a week. Her friend Connie had called the school, pretending to be her father, trying to get her reinstated, but the school did not believe he was who he said he was. It was Connie – Constantine – who finally convinced her she should tell me. Why did she conceal it? Did she think I would beat her? I never had. I'd rarely even raised my voice. I'd been disapproving and firm and most of all, worried, but I'd never struck her.

I asked her. She didn't know, she said. And I believed her. I don't think she knew what she was doing in those years. I went down to the school. Elspeth had said 'Jesus!' out loud in the gym class and the teacher had overheard it. That was the reason for the expulsion. Els had to apologise and I had to be present before they'd allow her to return to school.

The gym teacher, Miss Fahey, a red-haired woman in her fifties, lowered her voice as she explained her actions to me. There were two black girls in the corner

of her office, and she nodded towards them slightly. 'We expect that sort of language from *some* people,' she said, 'but not from *nice* girls like Elspeth.' Elspeth
110 stared at her with cold hate, said the required 'I'm sorry' like an automaton, then turned on her heel and left the room.

That summer, I took the children, and went to stay at my mother's house on the Cape. I felt I had to get Els
115 away from the environment that was making her destroy herself. She was listless all summer, but she got in no trouble. She read a lot. She wrote to Connie every day, and at the end of the summer, showed me the stack of letters she'd received from him. 'See, you
120 couldn't break us up after all,' she said with angry challenge on her face.

'What?'

'Connie and me. I know that's why you brought me out here.'

125 'Els, Connie has dinner at our house at least twice a week. Why would you think I was trying to break you up?'

'You wouldn't let Connie come out here.'

'You know why.'

130 My mother was terrified of black men, and would have gone into hysterics if Connie had merely visited. Even though Con was only a boy. She had no bad feelings about women and children of any colour, only the men.

135 'So?' Els said archly. 'It comes to the same thing, doesn't it?'

'If I wanted you to break up with Connie, I'd tell you so, Elspeth. You should know that.'

She grimaced and stormed off.

140 We returned to Cambridge.

But Elspeth was still miserable. Over the summer, Connie had got involved with another girl, and although he remained her best friend, was no longer available all the time. This was, of course, my fault. She
145 was over thirteen now, and began to go out at night, to dances. I gave her a deadline of one a.m., which she observed the first time, but not the second, and never again.

Marilyn French

Notes
1 Cambridge – Massachusets U.S.A.
2 M.I.T. – Massachusets Institute of Technology

THE BLEEDING HEART

FOR DISCUSSION OR WRITING

1 Do you think that Elspeth's mother deals with her daughter's behaviour adequately? If you do not, what action would you take?

2 If a child of yours was involved in (a) shoplifting and (b) taking drugs, what would you do to advise him? If your child ignored your advice would you involve the police?

3 If your parents did not approve of your choice of girl-friend/boy-friend would you end the relationship?

4 Do you know anyone who has been suspended from school? Did the crime merit the serious punishment?

5 As a parent what rules would you draw up for a thirteen year old child? Would they be the same rules for a girl and boy?

6 What punishment would you give Elspeth for ignoring the deadline you, her mother or father, had set? Do you think it would influence her behaviour the next time you allowed her out? If you were Elspeth what would your reaction to your mother's stand be? Write the dialogue you imagine took place when Elspeth came home at 1 a.m. You may wish to write the dialogue as a play.

COMPREHENSION

1 In what ways was Cambridge 'miles away in culture' from Newton? (5)

2 Why is the fact that the family moved to Cambridge in the late sixties relevant to the way Elspeth changed? (4)

3 What is Selene's attitude to Elspeth's mother? (3)

4 What is the 'puberty rite' (line 73) that Elspeth is carrying out? (2)

5 Two examples of the bigotry of the school administration are given. What are they? (2)

6 Why did the narrator decide to take her family to her mother's house on the Cape? (1)

7 Why did Elspeth think her mother was trying to destroy her relationship with Connie? (2)

8 What is the meaning of the following words as used in the passage:
   ethnic (line 9)
   encompass (line 44)
   bland-faced (line 76)
   automaton (line 111)
   listless (line 116)
   grimaced (line 139) (6)

'It's always the woman's fault.' I know in my head that this has to be nonsense. I was not expelled for doing anything very bad, and in the end was not so much expelled as let drop. But the headmaster's words still echo, and it is still easy for any man to make me feel guilty.

The High Anglican convent where I was a boarder – years ago, before the Flood – was keen on hand-loom weaving and Gregorian chant but not so good when it came to 'A' levels. So at the age of 17 I was sent to a boy's public school that took at that time very few girls and only in the sixth form. The contrast with the convent was so great that for the first few weeks I dared not look up, and saw nothing but forests of grey-flannel legs. This timidity was short-lived.

It was an unorthodox school, run by an unorthodox and brilliant headmaster known to staff and pupils as 'Bigwig'. His chief aide was his exquisitely groomed secretary, Miss Moody, who looked a bit like the Duchess of Windsor. Miss Moody's chief aide was a ferocious Alsatian dog called Boris.

Lessons were held in Nissen huts, and after school hours the more ambitious girls, under the pretext of needing peace and quiet to do their prep, would strategically station themselves in separate huts, sitting close to the windows through which we could see, and be seen by, the male talent strolling by: just like the ladies at their windows in the red-light district of Amsterdam, now I come to think of it.

The boys would go visiting in the huts of their choice, and if a girl pulled in the one she wanted, then love began. It was limited love, circumscribed by local conventions; just hours and hours of static kissing in an upright position behind the huts, and the right to the last dance at the monthly sixth-form 'hops'.

In my fifth term Jake joined the school: a huge, athletic, fair-haired 18-year-old South African: a beautiful blond beast. He prowled round the huts in the autumn dusk, while within their occupants trembled with anticipation. I wasn't very pretty and it seemed something of a miracle that Jake chose me. It went to my head.

At the hop, I agreed to Jake's suggestion that we should meet in the apple orchard afterwards. The girls lived in a cottage in the school garden; since I was head girl that term, it was up to me to see that everyone was safely in after the hop, and then lock up. I checked that everyone else was home, then slipped out to the dark orchard where the blond beast was waiting.

We were drowning in the statutory embrace when there was a sudden snuffle, and a rustle, and then loud barks. It was Boris, the Alsatian; and wherever Boris was, Miss Moody could not be far behind. We parted and fled. Boris was snapping at my heels as far as the cottage door. It was a dark night. Perhaps I hadn't been seen.

The next morning, I was summoned to Bigwig's study. I sat on the sofa. Bigwig paced up and down as he talked; behind him, her hands folded in her lap, sat Miss Moody, her sleek head bowed over her typewriter. At her feet lay horrible Boris. My crime, said Bigwig, was double: not only had I broken the rules, I had broken the rules that as head girl I was meant to enforce.

I was to be expelled. I was not to speak to Jake again, nor was I to canvass sympathy among my friends. Jake, however, was not going to be expelled. Why not? 'Because it's always the woman's fault.'

My mother wrote to me, 'You have been a fool,' which was about right. In the event I did not leave on the next train to London. I was due to take the Oxford entrance examination almost at once, and Bigwig conceded that I might stay until that was over. Since I had nothing to lose, Jake and I had further secret meetings which went undetected except by the games master, who did not report us.

My final departure was undramatic; I just sort of ebbed away at the end of term, under my dingy cloud. When it turned out that I had got into Oxford, Bigwig sent me a present of a sticky, crimson, sweet-tasting Charles of the Ritz lipstick.

Years later I saw Bigwig on television, happily asserting that he had never had to expel anyone from his school for boy-and-girl misdemeanours. He has forgotten all about me, I thought. (Or perhaps he reckoned that he had let me off.)

And what, precisely, is always the woman's fault? Everything that happens between the sexes, and especially everything that goes wrong, according to Bigwig. But when Adam tried the 'woman's fault' argument on God, a bigger bigwig, he took no notice and just expelled them both – from another apple orchard, rather before my time.

Victoria Glendinning
THE OBSERVER

LOVE BEHIND THE NISSEN HUTS
FOR DISCUSSION OR WRITING

1 What is your opinion of boarding schools? Would you like to go to one, or if you are a boarder are you glad that you were sent to one? Would you send your children to boarding school?

2 Give the arguments for and against private education.

3 Do you think mixed schools are a good idea or do you prefer the alternative of a single sex school? Give reasons for your answers.

4 Write an essay on the subject 'My First Date'.

5 'And what precisely is always the woman's fault? Everything that happens between the sexes, and especially everything that goes wrong.' In your experience, do girls always get the blame when there is trouble?

FLIGHT

Above the old man's head was the dovecote, a tall wire-netted shelf on stilts, full of strutting, preening birds. The sunlight broke on their grey breasts into small rainbows. His ears were lulled by their crooning,
5 his hands stretched up towards his favourite, a homing pigeon, a young plump-bodied bird which stood still when it saw him and cocked a shrewd bright eye.

'Pretty, pretty, pretty,' he said, as he grasped the bird and drew it down, feeling the cold coral claws
10 tighten around his finger. Content, he rested the bird lightly on his chest, and leaned against a tree, gazing out beyond the dovecote into the landscape of a late afternoon. In folds and hollows of sunlight and shade, the dark red soil, which was broken into great clods,
15 stretched wide to a tall horizon. Trees marked the course of the valley; a stream of rich green grass the road.

His eyes travelled homewards along this road until he saw his grand-daughter swinging on the gate
20 underneath a frangipani tree. Her fair hair fell down her back in a wave of sunlight, and her long bare legs repeated the angles of the frangipani stems, bare shining-brown stems among patterns of pale blossoms.

She was gazing, past the pink flowers, past the
25 railway cottage where they lived, along the road to the village.

His mood shifted. He deliberately held out his wrist for the bird to take flight, and caught it again at the moment it spread its wings. He felt the plump shape
30 strive and strain under his fingers; and, in a sudden access of troubled spite, shut the bird into the small box and fastened the bolt. 'Now you stay there,' he muttered and turned his back on the shelf of birds. He moved warily along the hedge, stalking his grand-
35 daughter, who was now looped over the gate, her head loose on her arms, singing. The light happy sound mingled with the crooning of the birds, and his anger mounted.

'Hey!' he shouted; saw her jump, look back, and
40 abandon the gate. Her eyes veiled themselves, and she said in a pert neutral voice: 'Hullo, Grandad.'

Politely she moved towards him, after a lingering backward glance at the road.

'Waiting for Steven, hey?' he said, his fingers curling
45 like claws into his palm.

'Any objection?' she asked lightly, refusing to look at him.

He confronted her, his eyes narrowed, shoulders hunched, tight in a hard knot of pain which included
50 the preening birds, the sunlight, the flowers, herself. He said: 'Think you're old enough to go courting, hey?' The girl tossed her head at the old-fashioned phrase and sulked, 'Oh Grandad!'

'Think you want to leave home, hey? Think you can
55 go running around the fields late at night?'

Her smile made him see her, as he had every evening of this warm end-of-summer month, swinging hand in hand along the road to the village with that red-handed, red-throated, violent-bodied youth, the
60 son of the postmaster. Misery went to his head and he shouted angrily: 'I'll tell your mother!'

'Tell away!' she said laughing, and went back to the gate. He heard her singing, for him to hear:

'I've got you under my skin,
65 I've got you deep in the heart of...'

'Rubbish,' he shouted. 'Rubbish. Impudent little bit of rubbish!'

Growling under his breath he turned towards the dovecote, which was his refuge from the house he
70 shared with his daughter and her husband and their children. But now the house would be empty. Gone all the young girls with their laughter and their squabbling and their teasing. He would be left, uncherished and alone, with that square-fronted, calm-eyed woman, his
75 daughter.

He stooped, muttering, before the dovecote, resenting the absorbed cooing birds.

From the gate the girl shouted: 'Go and tell! Go on, what are you waiting for?'
80 Obstinately he made his way to the house, with

quick, pathetic persistent glances of appeal back at her. But she never looked around. Her defiant but anxious young body stung him into love and repentance. He stopped. 'But I never meant...' he muttered, waiting for her to turn and run to him. 'I didn't mean...'

She did not turn. She had forgotten him. Along the road came the young man Steven, with something in his hand. A present for her? The old man stiffened as he watched the gate swing back, and the couple embrace. In the brittle shadows of the frangipani tree his grand-daughter, his darling, lay in the arms of the postmaster's son, and her hair flowed back over his shoulder.

'I see you!' shouted the old man spitefully. They did not move. He stumped into the little whitewashed house, hearing the wooden veranda creak angrily under his feet. His daughter was sewing in the front room, threading a needle held to the light.

He stopped again, looking back into the garden. The couple were now sauntering among the bushes, laughing. As he watched he saw the girl escape from the youth with a sudden mischievous movement, and run off through the flowers with him in pursuit. He heard shouts, laughter, a scream, silence.

'But it's not like that at all,' he muttered miserably. 'It's not like that. Why can't you see? Running and giggling, and kissing and kissing. You'll come to something quite different.'

He looked at his daughter with sardonic hatred, hating himself. They were caught and finished, both of them, but the girl was still running free.

'Can't you see?' he demanded of his invisible granddaughter, who was at that moment lying in the thick green grass with the postmaster's son.

His daughter looked at him and her eyebrows went up in tired forebearance.

'Put your birds to bed?' she asked, humouring him.

'Lucy,' he said urgently. 'Lucy...'

'Well what is it now?'

'She's in the garden with Steven.'

'Now you just sit down and have your tea.'

He stumped his feet alternately, thump, thump, on the hollow wooden floor and shouted: 'She'll marry him. I'm telling you, she'll be marrying him next!'

His daughter rose swiftly, brought him a cup, set him a plate.

'I don't want any tea. I don't want it, I tell you.'

'Now, now,' she crooned. 'What's wrong with it? Why not?'

'She's eighteen. Eighteen!'

'I was married at seventeen and I never regretted it.'

'Liar,' he said. 'Liar. Then you should regret it. Why do you make your girls marry? It's you who do it. What do you do it for? Why?'

'The other three have done fine. They've three fine husbands. Why not Alice?'

'She's the last,' he mourned. 'Can't we keep her a bit longer?'

'Come now, dad. She'll be down the road, that's all. She'll be here every day to see you.'

'It's not the same.' He thought of the other three girls, transformed inside a few months from charming petulant spoiled children into serious young matrons.

'You never did like it when we married?' she said. 'Why not? Every time, it's the same. When I got married you made me feel like it was something wrong. And my girls the same. You get them all crying and miserable the way you go on. Leave Alice alone. She's happy.' She sighed, letting her eyes linger on the sun-lit garden. 'She'll marry next month. There's no reason to wait.'

'You've said they can marry?' he said incredulously.

'Yes, dad, why not?' she said coldly, and took up her sewing.

His eyes stung, and he went out on the verandah. Wet spread down over his chin and he took out a handkerchief and mopped his whole face. The garden was empty.

From around a corner came the young couple; but their faces were no longer set against him. On the wrist of the postmaster's son balanced a young pigeon, the light gleaming on its breast.

'For me?' said the old man, letting the drops shake off his chin. 'For me?'

'Do you like it?' The girl grabbed his hand and swung on it. 'It's for you, Grandad. Steven brought it for you.' They hung about him, affectionate, concerned, trying to charm away his wet eyes and his misery. They took his arms and directed him to the shelf of birds, one on each side, enclosing him, petting him, saying wordlessly that nothing would be changed, nothing could change, and that they would be with him always. The bird was proof of it, they said, from their lying happy eyes, as they thrust it on him. 'There, Grandad, it's yours. It's for you.'

They watched him as he held it on his wrist, stroking its soft, sun-warmed back, watching the wings lift and balance.

'You must shut it up for a bit,' said the girl intimately. 'Until it knows this is its home.'

'Teach your grandmother to suck eggs,' growled the old man.

Released by his half-deliberate anger, they fell back, laughing at him. 'We're glad you like it.' They moved off, now serious and full of purpose, to the gate, where they hung, backs to him, talking quietly. More than anything could their grown-up seriousness shut him out, making him alone; also, it quietened him, took the sting out of their tumbling like puppies on the grass. They had forgotten him again. Well, so they should, the old man reassured himself, feeling his throat clotted with tears, his lips trembling. He held the new bird to his face, for the caress of its silken feathers. Then he shut it in a box and took out his favourite.

195 'Now you can go,' he said aloud. He held it poised, ready for flight, while he looked down the garden towards the boy and the girl. Then, clenched in the pain of loss, he lifted the bird on his wrist and watched it soar. A whirr and a spatter of wings, and a cloud of
200 birds rose into the evening from the dovecote.

At the gate Alice and Steven forgot their talk and watched the birds.

On the veranda, that woman, his daughter, stood gazing, her eyes shaded with a hand that still held her
205 sewing.

It seemed to the old man that the whole afternoon had stilled to watch his gesture of self-command, that even the leaves of the trees had stopped shaking.

Dry-eyed and calm, he let his hands fall to his sides
210 and stood erect, staring up into the sky.

The cloud of shining silver birds flew up and up, with a shrill cleaving of wings, over the dark ploughed land and the darker belts of trees and the bright folds of grass, until they floated high in the sunlight, like a cloud
215 of motes of dust.

They wheeled in a wide circle, tilting their wings so there was flash after flash of light, and one after another they dropped from the sunshine of the upper sky to shadow, one after another, returning to the valley and
220 the shelter of night.

The garden was all a fluster and a flurry of returning birds. Then silence, and the sky was empty.

The old man turned, slowly, taking his time; he lifted his eyes to smile proudly down the garden at his
225 grand-daughter. She was staring at him. She did not smile. She was wide-eyed, and pale in the cold shadow, and he saw the tears run shivering off her face.

Doris Lessing

1 When the story opens the pigeons were:
- **A** still and silent
- **B** still and noisy
- **C** moving and noisy
- **D** moving and silent

2 The old man's favourite pigeon (line 5) was:
- **A** intelligent
- **B** brightly coloured
- **C** thin
- **D** male

3 The grand-daughter (lines 20–23) is compared to:
- **A** sunshine
- **B** a tree
- **C** an animal
- **D** her grand-father

4 He tried (line 34) to:
- **A** approach quietly
- **B** to go away quietly
- **C** sing quietly
- **D** speak quietly

5 Talking to his grand-daughter, (lines 44–61) the old man became:
- **A** gentler
- **B** tired
- **C** cheerful
- **D** cross and upset

6 The old man's anger (lines 39–50) showed in all of these except ONE:
- **A** in his eyes
- **B** in his body
- **C** in his face
- **D** in his hands

7 His anger (lines 71–75) was caused by:
- **A** his dislike of his grand-daughter
- **B** his dislike of his son-in-law
- **C** his fear of his grand-daughter's friends
- **D** his fear of losing his grand-daughter

8 Further sight of the happy birds (line 76) made him:
- **A** happier
- **B** indifferent
- **C** thoughtful
- **D** indignant

9 As he returned home (lines 80–85) the old man felt:
- **A** persistent
- **B** regret for what he had said
- **C** angry
- **D** undecided about what to do

10 The old man's outbursts to his grand-daughter (lines 80–111) were caused by:
- **A** fear for her future
- **B** dislike of Steven
- **C** dislike of the girl
- **D** fear of his daughter

11 Lily spoke to her father (lines 116–117):
- **A** patiently
- **B** with surprise
- **C** sharply
- **D** amusingly

12 The old man did not want his grand-daughter to marry (lines 137–143) because:
- **A** she would be unhappy
- **B** she was young
- **C** she would change
- **D** she would move too far away

13 When the young people came back (lines 159–162) their expressions were:
- **A** hostile
- **B** rigid
- **C** friendly
- **D** hard

14 By their actions (lines 167–175) they tried:
- **A** to get round him
- **B** to reassure him

C to make him change his mind
D to stay with him

15 'Teach your grand-mother to suck eggs,' (line 181) as used here, means:
- **A** clear off
- **B** go and talk to his wife
- **C** give the pigeon to his wife
- **D** he knew a lot about pigeons

16 After the brief conversation (lines 183–186) the young people were:
- **A** relieved
- **B** mocking
- **C** afraid
- **D** indifferent

17 Letting the favourite pigeon go (lines 190–206) showed:
- **A** his loss of interest in the bird
- **B** it was time for its daily flight
- **C** his acceptance of the situation
- **D** he had forgotten the young people

18 The old man imagined (lines 206–208):
- **A** he was losing the pigeon
- **B** he was the centre of attention
- **C** no-one cared
- **D** everyone would obey him

19 When the birds had returned (lines 223–225) he:
- **A** admired his own behaviour
- **B** was proud of his grand-daughter
- **C** admired the birds
- **D** admired the sky

20 At the end of the story (lines 225–228) the girl was:
- **A** proud and happy
- **B** amused
- **C** cold
- **D** frightened and moved

FOOTBALLERS DON'T CRY

A dramatised version of Brian Glanville's short story

	(Phone rings. After a moment Peter picks it up)
PETER	(Startled) Hello, who's that?
DAD	(Upset) Peter, it's me. I –
PETER	Dad! What's up? It's late you know: it's one o'clock.
DAD	Peter, I've lost me job.
PETER	Dad – I'm sorry it's –
DAD	Called me in tonight and sacked me, they did.
PETER	Well, never you mind, there'll be summat else. Kick 'em back I say. Footballers don't cry, that's what you always told me.
DAD	Peter, I hope you'll never know what it's like to have this happen to you. To be stabbed in the back by a lot of fat, ungrateful businessmen who know nowt about football – and I've given my life to the game.
PETER	(Half asleep) Yes, Dad. I know, Dad.
	(Marion comes downstairs)
MARION	Who is it?
PETER	(Aside) It's Dad. He's just got the push.
MARION	Not again. It's the middle of the night. You're going to wake John.
PETER	Yeah. (Into phone) Dad?
DAD	Peter, are you there?
PETER	Yes. Look Dad. I'll phone you in the morning, right.
DAD	Oh . . . Aye, all right then.
PETER	God bless you, Dad. I'll phone you first thing tomorrow.
	(He replaces receiver. Baby starts crying upstairs)
PETER	Whew!
MARION	There now. You've woken John between you. What did I tell you . . .?
	(Fade)
PETER	I didn't sleep after that. I lay awake, thinking of all he'd done for me, and how much I'd always admired him . . . Just a little lad going to watch him play at Bolton and at Rotherham. Then later on, when he dropped out of the league, at Wigan and Boston and Kettering. Get in, Dad! Go on, Dad. Centre-half, a great big fellow coming in bang with his thick legs, ploughing through the mud with his sliding tackles, and always first to the ball, a hard man, tough, brave, strong, a bit dirty; though I never thought that, then.
DAD	You'll be a winger, Peter. Come on, left foot, right foot, move it!
PETER	(Breathless) Hang on, Dad! All I wanted was to be a centre-half, like him . . . Later, there were all the piddling little jobs he had, coach this, manager of that, of nothing. Clubs always in debt, playing in front of a few hundred people and him having to do everything, mark out the pitch, treat the injuries.
DAD	Peter, *you're* my answer, son. When you make it, I'll make it. The war did me, Peter, as a player. Took the best years of my career away. I'd have played for England, then there'd have been no stopping me. Manager of Arsenal, manager of Everton. I've done miracles with rubbish. But you get no medals for that.
PETER	And he hadn't. He'd last three months here, six months there, then something would snap, he'd quarrel with the Chairman, blow his top to the Press, even thump one of the players, and out he'd go.
DAD	But you, Peter, you will justify me. By your career. By your skill. And then they will begin to see that I practise what I preach! Through my own son, who *nobody* can say I did not develop. You'll never disappoint me, Peter. I know that.
PETER	And I knew it too: I'd rather have cut my leg off . . . I was more chuffed when he got to be manager of City than when I first played, came to London for Rovers, and then England. Things were like they should be again. It wasn't me getting two hundred quid a week while he got forty and much too proud to accept owt any more. So, after breakfast, while Marion was feeding the baby, we talked about what we were going to do.
	(Baby gurgles)
PETER	. . . You just don't know football, Marion.
MARION	I know him and I know you. He always wants you to be a little puppet dancing to his strings. He's not coming to stay is he?
PETER	I don't know. What else can I say? Just till he gets settled – till he gets another job. He's shattered, Marion.
MARION	He'll shatter us . . .
PETER	He was in a right state when he got to us. All tense and taut, that twitch at the side of his mouth.

	DAD	Hello, Marion.
	MARION	Hello, Dad.
105	DAD	By, things have changed a bit since I were playing. This place must be worth thirty thousand. In my day it was eight pounds a week and a pint at the boozer.
	PETER	Mm.
110	DAD	Well! Now let's wait for the offers to come pouring in.
	PETER	Oh, it's early days yet, Dad.
	DAD	Oh, yes. I don't expect them to come rushing... You don't think there'd be something for me at the Rovers?
115		
	PETER	What? Oh, well there might be, Dad. Not as Manager, just now, nor as coach. Bobby Birchall's doing both.
	DAD	I know, I didn't mean that.
120	PETER	Well ... what else is there? Looking after the Reserves?
	DAD	Maybe I could help with the coaching and the scouting. Something like that. (Almost pleading) Weighing up teams they're going to play?
125		
	PETER	(Embarrassed) I'll try tomorrow. I'll see Geoff Creamer ... (Fade)
	PETER	... Just a bit of scouting and coaching to be going on with, Geoff. It's shattered him, this, I think maybe he needs to get his confidence back.
130		
	GEOFF	There's not much for him here, Peter. Not for *him*. I'll talk to the Chairman...
135	PETER	I could tell Geoff was uneasy. Well, he didn't want to upset me, and at the same time he obviously knew about Dad, his reputation... A couple of days later he called me in.
140	GEOFF	... Pete, we've got something for your father, on the lines he asked for. I'm afraid we can't pay him a lot – it's just a port in a storm you know... (Fade)
145	PETER	So he started with them just like he'd wanted, going to look at teams and players for the Boss, taking individual players for special skills where we trained, nice and near my home. Of course I was very glad for him – but it made things strange, him being at the club, him living at my house. Marion could hardly keep quiet.
150		
	MARION	I don't know how you put up with it. Treating you like a baby, and he wouldn't have a job if it weren't for you.
155		
	PETER	I know. That's why I put up with it.
	MARION	Every day he says, 'I mustn't burden you. I'll find a room in a hotel.' Well look, if I hear

160		that once more I'll go out and find one for him.
	PETER	I know ... I know it's not easy, love... (Crossfade)
	DAD	... like that game when you were losing at home to Newcastle. Then look how you missed that penalty. Go low and angled, low and angled, Peter. How many more times do I have to tell you that?... (Fade)
165		
	PETER	And then it started at the club. I knew it would do. First he didn't reckon the Coach, Bobby Birchall. But then he never reckoned any coach, especially the one that was coaching me. He'd be out on the field when Bobby was working with us, shaking his head, clicking his tongue, till it was so obvious that Bobby noticed and naturally he didn't like it. One day Geoff had me in the office.
170		
175		
	GEOFF	Look Peter, you'll have to talk to your father. We're glad to have him here till he gets something else, but he must realise that Bobby Birchall is coach; and I'm the Manager.
180		
	PETER	I know. It's so difficult for Dad. He's used to helping me.
185		
	GEOFF	Yes, well just a quiet word. I shouldn't like anything to go wrong... (Fade)
	PETER	Of course, I didn't talk to Dad; how could I? He'd no time for Bobby, and even less for the Boss.
190		
	DAD	They'll burn you out this club. They want you on both bloody wings; and fetching and carrying in midfield. I'm going to have a word with Geoff Creamer. I'll tell him –
195		
	PETER	Please don't Dad. I can tell him myself.
	DAD	Ay, but you haven't, have you? It's just as well I'm here... (Fade)
200	PETER	The trouble was, there was truth in what he said... The big blow-up came when we played Milan in the first leg of the European Cup at our place. Everything went wrong in the first half. At half-time Bobby and Geoff came into the dressing-room with the old man. Bobby and the Boss just stood there like a couple of dummies, but my old man leapt right in. (Changing room background)
205		
210	DAD	Well if you two haven't got anything to say, I have. I've never seen such a pathetic exhibition. You're playing right into their hands. No skill, no method... (Fade)

215 PETER He was still at full blast when the buzzer went for the second-half. The thing was that his pep talk worked. I think that's what they couldn't forgive him for. We equalised, and very nearly won. After the match the Boss
220 didn't show in the dressing room at all, just Bobby looking a bit sheepish, and the old man.
(Changing room)

DAD That was better, lads, if you'd played like
225 that the whole of the game, you'd have bloody annihilated them!

PETER But all I kept wondering was where the Boss was, and what he was saying to the Chairman. There was what you might call
230 an atmosphere. The word went round that a few of the lads were going to a night-club. I asked Dad if he'd like to come along.
(Changing room)

DAD A night club? After a game like this? If

you'd been trying, you'd all be too tired to
235 do anything but go to bed.

PETER Well I'm going, Dad. I'll see you later.

DAD (Going) You little tyke.
(Fade)

240 PETER I got home late. The light was still on in the front room. He was sitting there with his head in his hands. I'd never seen him look so shattered, his eyes all red, he looked a hundred years old.

245 DAD (Tearful) They've sacked me, Peter.

PETER I'm sorry Dad.

DAD Sorry! Is that all you can say? You're not going to stay there, are you? You'll ask for a transfer?

250 PETER ... No, Dad.
Get up, I thought, get up; footballers don't cry. I knew he'd never get up now.

Brian Glanville

FOOTBALLERS DON'T CRY
FOR DISCUSSION OR WRITING

1 Pretend you are Marion. Write a letter to your sister in which you tell her of the changes which have taken place since Peter's father has come to live with you, or write the telephone conversation between you and your sister in which you air your grievances.

2 What is your opinion of Peter's father interfering in both Peter's private and personal life? When you marry do you think parents' responsibilities to you end?

3 Have parents the right to try to live out their hopes through their children?

4 Have your parents a particular hobby or pastime which they have encouraged you to share? Explain what the hobby is, how you became interested and why you would recommend it to others.

5 Some day you may have to look after an aged parent. Would you allow the parent to live with your family or would you find an Old People's Home for him or her?

DILEMMAS

DILEMMAS

They hang in hundreds, fifteen rows of them, each on a numbered peg. The reception area, the foyer of this stern Edwardian block, is a shower of purple azaleas. Two receptionists sit at a switchboard. It could be any institution, except for those keys and their guardian. A burly figure in blue shirt and dark-blue trousers, he looks like a prison officer. This is Rampton special hospital; he is a nurse.

We cross the foyer, through glass doors into a short corridor. From a door on the left, more nurses in regulation blue macs are hurrying in from the rain. The day shift. On the right is a plain green door with no handle and three locks. Rampton is our society's ultimate dustbin. This door is its lid.

My escorts beyond it are the hospital administrator, Derek Atha – his keys hang, chatelaine fashion, from two belts – and Ken Scott, a portly, fresh-faced man who is one of Rampton's seven senior nursing officers, each in charge of several wards. Scott has been here for 30 years – 'almost as long as any patient,' he observes.

Mary Ward, 7.50 a.m.: Sister May Simpson, a tiny Scot, arrives to relieve the night nurse. A Rampton ward, one to each floor of a block, is not a dormitory but a corridor of cells, 'side-rooms' they call them. At one end a day-room for the patients, at the other the charge-nurse's office.

Shoes line the Mary Ward corridor outside each door. The 'girls' – everyone calls them girls, though Mary Ward's 15 patients range in physical age from 25 to 50 – have been quiet since 11 p.m., most of them sedated with anything from Valium to Largactil or Sparine. Every quarter of an hour, the night nurse has peeped through the two-by-two spyhole in each door at the three 'disturbed' girls who were 'in seclusion' – locked in – the day before.

Sister Simpson goes through the routine: reads the night report, checks the drugs given, does a body count, signs for the inmates. Then she counts her nurses. Mary Ward's patients are judged psychopathic or subnormal; 12 of the 15 are on indefinite restriction orders: the rule is that six nurses must be on duty before their doors may be opened. 'I've got the right number now,' Sister says, harassed. 'But they don't know the girls. The girls need someone to relate to. If they keep things to themselves they'll just explode.'

She knocks and open each door, goes in. A nursing assistant, in green – clearly the woman whose experience she most trusts – waits outside, out of sight, but within earshot. Two going in might startle a patient.

Slowly the women shuffle out in their nightwear, carrying grey cardboard potties. (The three who were difficult yesterday will be let out later.) They go to sister's office to get their locker keys, make-up and lavatory paper. In the bathroom opposite even the taps have keys.

'Look!' – a patient points in friendly fashion to the wording on Sister's coffee mug: 'I hate people who sing in the mornings.' Down the ward corridor someone is crying. There is a sudden screech; Janet is teasing Brenda.

Sister is still worried: 'You've got to be careful with young nurses, they have very little experience. One of mine, for instance, has a rather prim way of speaking that has annoyed a paranoid schizophrenic. She has told me how this nurse makes her feel; but the nurse will now have to be careful, and she may not grasp this at all.

'It's the little things that wouldn't necessarily bother a normal person that trigger off explosions. If it's a sunny day, most will be in a good mood. But for one extremely paranoid girl, the sunshine can be saying bad things to her; and a chronic neurotic will be moaning that everything is black and she feels genuinely suicidal.'

Sister Simpson's husband works at Rampton, and she chats to the patients about her home life: 'I try to show them what they are missing in the outside world and why it is worth trying. Coming from Rampton they will be ostracised anyway; but if they are clean and tidy and fit in a social sense they are more likely to stay out after release. But put one foot wrong and they will be sent straight back.

'Society demands that they are put behind bars and then says "poor things". The hypocrisy goes further. Let them back out and society will moan and groan again. Society puts them here and society sends them back again.'

I use the Mary Ward lavatory; a nurse would have her own key but, for safety, I am locked in. From the yard below comes a dreadful weeping, wailing braying which breaks into sporadic chattering. I crane to see what is going on but the bars block my view. I have a sudden sense of imprisonment here. In time the noise dies away.

Rampton has excellent workshops: a shoe shop, tailor's shop, bakehouse, carpentry hall, pottery. The men of D-block cannot use them. They are judged too unstable. The most dangerous male patients of all are here in Drake ward: men from other wards are brought here in crisis; 14 of its 24 beds are occupied by patients in violent spell. The six staff on duty here observe two cardinal rules: keep your back to the wall and always stay in sight of another nurse.

The memory of Carstairs hangs over Rampton. Carstairs is Rampton's Scottish counterpart; in November

1976 two psychopaths broke out, killing a staff nurse and a patient and, before recapture, hacking to death a policeman. Now, apart from those line-of-sight pre-
110 cautions, the survival drill for any Rampton nurse is somehow to get to a telephone long enough to dial 222, which brings help running from all directions.

So I sit in the Drake ward office, looking at the patients in the day-room through a sheet of armoured
115 glass. Through it, muffled, come shouts and yells from the day-room: a disturbed and subnormal man is making a fuss. Two patients are 'secluded' in their cubicles: the blankets there are unrippable nylon duvets. In the centre of the room a man diagnosed as a
120 psychopath – but so convinced there is nothing wrong with him that he refused psychiatric help – pushes an electric floor-polisher with meticulous precision...

Pills are the staff of life in Rampton: without them life would seemingly be intolerable, insupportable for
125 many there. But a price is paid. Charge-nurse Prest summons a 20-year-old into his office to talk to me. The young man says he would rather be in prison: 'At least there I would be shut away.' I must have looked puzzled. There are too many in Rampton he wanted to
130 strangle, he says.

He is on Modecate, a tranquilliser heavy enough to cope with psychoses. The drug had dispelled 'the dead bodies and guts' which had enveloped him night and day since he was 16, gone too was the vision that
135 people's heads were on fire. What he now has, as a side-effect night and day, is trembling hands.

The men are keen to talk. One shows me his poem to 'a mother' – not *his* mother. Another, a Jew, shows me his drawings – black looming vultures, jump-jets,
140 German soldiers dying bloodily – and a letter to an MP, full of references to the persecutions of the Jews and mysterious people sticking needles in his heart. Later, in his office, Prest hands me a bundle of previous letters: 'They've asked us to stop him. So he writes, I
145 hold the letters, the MP doesn't get them any more.

The MP said: "You are the institution; do something to protect me".'

Upstairs again, on the third floor of D-block, I am due, at my own request, to lunch with the patients. But
150 when I sit at the table I find I can't go through with it. Inventing hurried excuses, I feel suddenly guilty when I notice that all the men trooping in have specially cleaned their shoes. I find myself appalled, taking comfort in the fact that they were probably made to...
155 'The staff here are asked to cope with very difficult, sometimes very nasty people, and to treat them as human beings. This they must find very difficult to do, even after training.'

I am talking to Dr. Ian Pickering, chairman of the
160 hospital consultants and, until 1976, medical adminis-trator at the Home Office. He goes on: 'Staff have even said to me, "We are dealing with human dross here, the bottom of the barrel, scum". Which is a very telling reflection of their feelings – inner feelings.
165 'I think Carstairs 1976 had a profound psychological effect on the nurses, and still has,' he says. And when we discuss the day-to-day violence of the patients, he adds: 'I'm sure this has a wear-and-tear effect on the staff, particularly when patients get to feel they have
170 been in Rampton too long and would have been out earlier if the judge had sent them to prison instead. That sense of frustration can turn into hatred.

'In a large number of cases, the patients are right. They do stay here too long. And of course as a doctor
175 I'm a bit peeved when my opinion about a patient's possible discharge is not taken up. But, as a person, I understand the reluctance of the authorities.

'I don't think we should ever take away a patient's hope that he or she will be discharged. I think patients
180 sometimes invent little reasons of their own to keep living. But in many cases, hope is a bit of an illusion.'

Alison Miller
THE SUNDAY TIMES

INSIDE RAMPTON

FOR DISCUSSION OR WRITING

1 Sister Simpson says, 'society puts them here and society sends them back again,' (line 87). Do you agree with her statement? Can society be accused of 'put(ting) them here'?

2 Why do you think the euphemisms 'in seclusion' and 'secluded' (lines 35 and 117) are used?

3 Why does Dr. Pickering feel that 'in many cases, hope is a bit of an illusion' (line 181) for the patients in Ramptom?

4 Did this description of the day-to-day life in a mental hospital shock you? If so, why?

5 'You are the institution; do something to protect me' wrote the M.P. to the authorities at Rampton (line 146). Write in full the formal letter you think this M.P. would have sent to Rampton.

6 A nurse loses his/her patience and hits one of the patients. Using the information given by Sister Simpson and Dr. Pickering write a defence of the nurse's action.

1 What signifies that Rampton is different from most large buildings? (2)

2 Explain the following lines: 'Rampton is our society's ultimate dustbin. This door is its lid.' (line 13) (2)

3 What punishments did the three 'disturbed' girls receive? (2)

4 What is one of the duties of the night nurse? (1)

5 What are the first duties of the sister who comes on for the day shift? (5)

6 Why does Sister Simpson accuse society of hypocrisy? (lines 85–88) (3)

7 Why are young nurses particularly vulnerable in Rampton? (2)

8 How does the sister try to encourage her patients? (3)

9 Explain the meaning of the following as used in the passage:
ultimate (line 13)
sedated (line 32)
subnormal (line 41)
chronic (line 73)
ostracised (line 80) (5)

I AM

I am: what I am none cares or knows,
  My friends forsake me like a memory lost;
I am the self-consumer of my woes,
  They rise and vanish in oblivion lost,
5 Like shades in love or death's oblivion lost;
  And yet I am, and live with shadows lost.

Into the nothingness of scorn and noise,
  Into the living sea of waking dreams,
Where there is neither sense of life nor joys,
10 But the vast shipwreck of my life's esteems;
And e'en the dearest – that I loved the best –
Are strange – nay, rather stranger than the rest.

I long for scenes where man has never trod,
  A place where woman never smiled or wept;
15 There to abide with my Creator, God,
  And sleep as I in childhood sweetly slept;
Untroubling and untroubled where I lie,
The grass below – above the vaulted sky.

John Clare

**I AM
FOR DISCUSSION OR WRITING**

1 Does this poem give you a good insight into the feelings and thoughts of someone who has lost his sanity?

2 In the third verse Clare offers a picture of his ideal retreat. Do you think it significant that this sanctuary is outside society and that he feels this is the place where he can be 'untroubling' and 'untroubled'?

SNOWY
FOR DISCUSSION OR WRITING

Snowy has raised thousands of pounds for charity through his own colourful personality and his cart full of all sorts of animals.

1 In what other ways do people raise money for charity? Have you taken part in any fund raising activities?
2 Do you give freely to people collecting money for charity or do you ever refuse? Give reasons for your answer.
3 Do you think that contributions to charity from Income Tax should be obligatory? Give reasons for your answer.
4 It is now a cliché to say that the British care more about the treatment of animals than that of children. Do you agree with this statement? Give reasons for your answer.
5 Which charity would you give most support to? Why?

'The hostel I live in isn't exactly the Savoy but to a destitute ex-con it's a godsend. The team who administer the place are young and extremely dedicated. They need to be. Looking after a house full of social misfits requires stamina and extraordinary tolerance. And saintly patience. For many ex-prisoners these youngsters represent their first real contact with normal human beings.

My return to freedom was like a space-traveller setting foot on some strange planet: a great many changes had taken place during my absence. London was Bedlam. My brain couldn't accommodate the riotous new sights and colours. I was frightened to talk to people. For the first few days I didn't dare venture outdoors. I ate alone in my room. I considered suicide. The hostel staff were kind and understanding. I don't think I could have survived without their support and encouragement.

A typical day starts around seven a.m. I'll spend the first few minutes luxuriating in bed, smoking a cigarette and musing on my unaccustomed liberty. I'll lie there and marvel over the simple things I can do – opening and closing a door, making independent decisions, being rude or polite, as and when the mood takes me. It seems almost incredible that I can actually express myself without fear. At the back of my mind there is pity for the poor sods I've left behind.

I slosh my face and then descend to the communal kitchen in the basement. A quick cup of tea and I'm back in my room preparing for the frustrating task of searching for work.

Few employers are willing to take a chance with an ex-con. But who knows? Today I might strike lucky.

By mid-day I'm feeling footsore and depressed. I've come up against the age-barrier. I'm 52 and it shows. My face is ravaged from years of dissipation and neglect. My health is still tolerably good but a prolonged penal diet plays havoc with a man's constitution. I'm paunchy and unprepossessing. I'm also self-conscious about my appearance because my clothes are unfashionable and showing signs of wear. At interviews my nervousness creates the wrong impression.

A quick assessment of my finances permits me to slip into a cafe for a fortifying cup of tea. My paltry allowance from the DHSS doesn't stretch to a packet of biscuits or a sandwich; I seem to exist on eggs, baked beans and the occasional meat pie. How is a man supposed to survive on £38.10 per week? I'm usually skint after four or five days.

I try to economise by walking instead of taking a bus or tube, but trudging to and fro wears my shoeleather dangerously thin. Small wonder my demoralised state is all too apparent to a prospective employer.

At six I'm back in the hostel. I listen to some of the other chaps bitching about their own misfortunes. It simply isn't true that shared miseries are made lighter. Hearing the woes of others only increases my sense of isolation and bitterness.

One of the hostel staff greets me with a warm smile and invites me to join her for a cigarette and a friendly chat. I pour out my troubles. Within a few minutes I'm relaxed and my weariness evaporates. I'm the sort of person who needs constant reassurance. The hostel staff obviously sense my anxiety and they flatter me with a little extra attention.

When I'm really pushed for funds they'll slip me a couple of quid... My sentence stripped me of my pride and my self-respect. There was a time when I would rather have died than accept a handout. Now I open my palm with alacrity.

In an attempt to create a homely atmosphere the hostel staff occasionally prepare a communal dinner. The girls are excellent cooks. The more domesticated residents assist with the washing-up and afterwards all retire to the lounge to watch a pre-war movie on the telly. But the television set is old and keeps developing faults. Exasperated, I adjourn to the privacy of my room where I bash away at an even more decrepit typewriter.

In a former Avatar[1] I was a moderately successful freelance journalist. I'm trying to regain my long-neglected fluency, but I'm out of practice and my style is torpid and uninspiring. Still, my rejected material is usually accompanied by a sympathetic letter and a convincing invitation to submit further examples. I'm heartened.

It's nearly midnight and I'm still busy at the typewriter. I'm distracted by a gurgling radiator. I'm tired and hungry; I won't be able to sleep without something to eat. I knock on my neighbour's door and beg some bread and cheese. We spend a few minutes discussing job prospects and I learn of some part-time work in a local pub.

I worry about references. I've reached the stage where I lie easily about my background. Henceforth I'm a recently-returned exile from Australia. A plausible falsehood to which my fast-fading Parkhurst suntan adds verisimilitude. The night hours pass slowly and when I rise from my writing table the darkened sky is streaked with light. A new day. I wonder what it is going to bring?

Jack Jacobs
SUNDAY TIMES MAGAZINE

Note
1 Avatar – incarnation – life

WHEN BLACK TURNS WHITE

Eddie Mae Kearney sits in the tiny kitchen of her rented basement in the suburbs of Westbury, an hour's drive from the skyscrapers of Manhattan. It is stifling. The central-heating boiler for the whole wooden house 5 hisses and steams. Bare pipes line the walls. Upstairs someone is boiling up pigs' trotters; the smell wafts down.

A door leads to a bedroom just large enough to accommodate a bed and the black-and-white tele- 10 vision on which Eddie Mae watches, day in, day out, the soap operas which are her only escape from the baffling reality of her life.

Beyond the back door there is a small patch of garden, left untended because her pale skin is suscep- 15 tible to sunburn and her weak eyes are sensitive to the light.

Eddie Mae brings out family snapshots, points out her parents back home in Georgia in the Deep South. Her pretty young daughters with their mother – a 20 white-haired, white-skinned woman with negro features. And herself as a teenager, attractive and black.

She was 18 when she was taken into hospital to be treated for tuberculosis. After a series of antibiotics her 25 skin began to turn blacker. Then, during an operation, her heart stopped. Doctors fought to save her. She was in intensive care, semi-conscious, for three weeks. During that time, her skin began to crack and peel, shedding to reveal white skin underneath.

30 'When I came to,' she recalls, 'and I started looking around me, the first thing I saw was my hands. They were white. I looked at my body, and it was white. I started screaming. They wouldn't bring me a mirror, they just put me to sleep again.'

35 When she recovered full consciousness on November 10, 1959, she saw what the doctors at Nassau County Medical Centre, New York, had recorded: 'Young coloured female with TB, exfoliated dermatitis following drugs, causing patient to be de- 40 pigmented.' Not only was her skin white; so was her hair.

'It was,' says Eddie Mae with stark understatement, 'a shock to everyone.' Her mother was shattered, her two babies didn't recognise her, one of her sisters, 45 fearful that the disease was contagious, refused to see her. And her husband, from whom she was already separated, never saw her again.

For more than 20 years she felt outfaced by the problem of adjusting to being a black woman in a 50 white woman's skin, and only now is she beginning to find some salvation.

At first she hid herself from the world. She didn't work, rarely went out except to her doctor and to the hospital, or to see her family down South, and then she 55 covered herself from head to toe. She wore wigs, dyed her hair. Black children ridiculed her in the street, adults insulted her. When she was turned away from a blacks-only restaurant in her native Georgia ('we don't serve no whites in here,' she was told) the irony of her 60 situation was complete.

It was a long time before, encouraged by her little girls, she ventured out into the world. In time she even started going out with men. 'A couple of them were white. They didn't know I was any different. They 65 freaked out when they saw my kids.'

In 1979 she thought the fervent prayers of 20 years had been answered, when she woke one morning to find her hands were beginning to turn black. Further inspection confirmed it; black spots were appearing all 70 over her body.

Only they stayed that way – as ugly black marks. Her fingers, the palms of her hands, her feet were black; she had spots on her forehead, nose, mouth, chin, arms and legs.

75 'I was afraid to look at myself in the mirror.It got so I would only go out to see the doctor, and even then I'd be smothered in clothes like an eskimo, I was so ashamed.'

For three years she suffered acutely while scientists 80 and doctors at Yale University, New Haven, Connecticut, tried to find a cure. Most of the medical experts she has seen believe she is suffering from vitiligo, a condition that strips away the body's pigment. It is thought to be an auto-immune disease, one in which 85 the body turns against some of its own cells and destroys them. It can be set off by allergy – in her case probably the allergy to antibiotics – and it may go with some other possibly auto-immune disease such as pernicious anaemia. It may affect the hair as well as the 90 skin, and is difficult to diagnose with any certainty.

Indeed, Eddie Mae says she has been told by Yale scientists that vitiligo is *not* to blame for her condition. 'They say they don't know what's wrong with me, they're still trying to find the cause and the cure. Last 95 time I was there I had 150 scientists looking me up and down. They gave me some cream to put on.'

The bleaching cream is Eddie Mae's tube of magic. Two months after she started using it, her fingers turned white again, the black spots began to disap-100 pear. But when she stops using the cream, the spots start to reappear, and often she can't find, out of her social security money, the $11.35 a tube she needs every week.

At times she's very lonely. Her daughters, now aged 105 25 and 26, have joined the armed services. Only three of her eight brothers and sisters keep in touch with her – one brother converted the basement of a house he owns into a home for her – and one sister in particular still thinks her condition is contagious. 'I used to go and 110 stay with her, but then I heard she would sterilise my plate and knife and fork after I left.'

Once she came close to suicide. 'I was very depressed – not bitter, just really unhappy. My parents were dead by then, my kids had gone and I was by 115 myself. My mind told me to jump out of the fifth-floor window. I was praying and praying and crying and hanging out of the window. Then I found myself back in bed. I didn't have no family near me to say "You're all right", to say something for comfort. I didn't have 120 nobody.'

These days she does have 'the lady upstairs, a couple of old friends and Barbara Castagna and Josephine Sorrentino at the doctor's office. They talk to me a lot, tell me not to be ashamed.'

125 Her doctor, a colourful, gargantuan man, believes she has a rare, extreme case of vitiligo. 'There's nothing much I can do for her,' he says realistically, 'except to give her my time every couple of weeks; I talk to her, comfort her. We haven't been treating her 130 with any special medication, just making her more comfortable with tranquillisers to help her cope with things a little better.

'Hardly anyone has done any research into this condition because it is so rare. People have just learned to 135 live with it. There was no specific treatment for the depigmented area in the Sixties. It meant Eddie Mae's life changed. She is not accepted by the black community and she is certainly not going to be accepted by the white community.'

140 But slowly things are beginning to look brighter. 'She's adjusting to it,' says Dr. Scheiner. 'This notoriety and attention she's getting is replacing her anxiety, and she's become a heroine. She's living with it.'

Dr. Scheiner thinks that the treatment she received 145 for her respiratory disease, or the X-rays she underwent, may have caused a hormonal disturbance, and all the pigment was just withdrawn from each individual cell. Medically, he says, there is very little hope that her black colour will ever return. 'I've observed 150 her for the past year, since she started turning black, and her condition now seems to be stabilised. She's as white as I am, and I think that's the way she will stay. I've never seen a case like hers before. She's unique.'

In our society we talk of 'black' and 'white', but in 155 reality only albinos are truly white. The rest of us have skins darkened by a dye, melanin, buried deep in the skin. The amount of melanin is fixed by heredity, and a number of genes control skin colour, so it can vary from the very pale skin of the Celt to the deep black of 160 the African. The colour of the black races is deepened by black cells called melanocytes in the surface skin.

All of which is of little concern to Eddie Mae. She knows only that she was 'black' and is not 'white', unacceptable to both black and white communities, a 165 curiosity to people of every hue. And she knows what colour she would *like* to be.

Her features are still those of a black woman, she lives in a black community, her friends and family are black. She dyes her hair black, wears make-up to 170 darken her skin. And she always wears dark glasses to protect her light-sensitive eyes.

'I feel strange. I don't seem to fit in. I don't know what to say to people when they stop me and say, "What is that?" I tell them that I was born black and I *am* black, 175 but they look at me kinda funny.

'When my daughters were little, people used to ask me if I was looking after them for their mother. That used to hurt me so.

'And kids have been little rats to me. Once, the day 180 Martin Luther King died, about 13 black teenage kids followed me to my door, cursing me and calling me names, calling me a white bitch. I told them I was black, but they laughed at me. A girl kicked me, she called me all white names. I was crying.

185 'Two weeks later the girl came to my house with my daughters. She didn't know I was their mother. I wanted to hit her, but the look on her face stopped me.

'One of my worst moments ever was seeing my Daddy again, years after I turned white. He was still 190 living in Georgia. He saw me – he was so shocked – but he held out his hands to me and I ran to him and hugged him.

'I still pray that one day I will wake up and be as black as my beautiful daughters, as black as my 195 mother. She died a few years ago, still tortured by what happened to me.

'My daughters have totally accepted me, they don't know no difference. When they were little they used to say, "Mommy why are you white and we're black?" I 200 didn't know what to tell them. They used to get a big kick out of inviting their friends home and introducing me to them. I'd hear them whispering, their friends would go into shock.'

So life goes on in that hot stuffy basement, with the 205 television flickering in the corner, the boiler hissing and steaming, the weeds overrunning the back yard.

'But one day life will be better than this. Lord, I really hope so!'

Eddie Mae thinks her story would make an interest-210 ing TV movie, and is hoping to sell the idea to a Hollywood producer who has contacted her. She has also struck up a bizarre pen-pal relationship with a young black prisoner, who saw her when she appeared on television to talk about her condition.

215 'Look at these pictures he keeps sending me.' She shuffles the snapshots on the kitchen table. They show a muscle-man posing, body-beautiful. 'Isn't he a fine-looking young man? He's asked me to marry him, but I don't think it's me he's after – I think he thinks I'm going 220 to make some money out of a TV movie. Well, look at me. Who's going to take a chance on me? Tomorrow I might wake up and be another person.'

Rachel Griggs
OBSERVER MAGAZINE

WHEN BLACK TURNS WHITE
FOR DISCUSSION OR WRITING

1 Do you think that Eddie Mae's story would 'make an interesting T.V. Movie'? Give reasons for your answer.

2 Write three scenes for such a 'T.V. Movie' which would reveal some details of her life from 1969 to the present day. Incorporate some of the real life situations described in the article.

3 Do you think Eddie Mae has coped well with 'the baffling reality of her life'? Has she shown any characteristics that you admire?

4 Can you think of any other 'changes' which could radically affect someone's life? Choose such an event and tell the story either
(a) leading up to and including the 'change' or
(b) of the 'change' and what happened after it occurred.

WHEN BLACK TURNS WHITE
Lines 1–131   MULTIPLE CHOICE COMPREHENSION

1 In the opening paragraph the author is suggesting that Eddie Mae Kearney's home is:
A comfortable
B well heated
C conveniently situated
D depressing

2 'Trotters' (line 6) are:
A meat
B feet
C heads
D legs

3 The word nearest in meaning to 'baffling' (line 12) is:
A helpless
B depressing
C unexpected
D bewildering

4 The word 'susceptible' (line 14) as used in the passage, means:
A sensitive
B used to
C exposed
D indifferent

5 From paragraph 3 we may infer that she gardens:
A lovingly
B never
C often
D in fine weather

6 The photographs (line 17) show:
A how many daughters she had
B how young she still looked
C the change in her appearance
D how pretty she still was

7 Her sister (line 44) would not meet her because:
  A she was ashamed
  B she thought she would suffer a similar fate
  C she was too ill
  D she was shocked

8 Her experience at the restaurant (line 58) was one:
  A she would not have expected in other circumstances
  B she could not believe
  C she found too hard to bear
  D she laughed at

9 'they freaked out' (line 65) is an expression which is:
  A facetious
  B exaggerated
  C colloquial
  D sarcastic

10 She prayed (line 66)
  A continuously
  B ardently
  C occasionally
  D feverishly

11 'Pigment' (line 83) is:
  A skin
  B a disease
  C colouring matter
  D sunburn

12 Another word for 'pernicious' (line 88) is:
  A severe
  B continuous
  C permanent
  D ordinary

13 It is difficult to diagnose vitiligo. Line 90 refers to the fact that:
  A it is rarely seen
  B it is difficult to identify it
  C it is hard to see it
  D it goes away quickly

14 'Bleaching cream' (line 97):
  A darkens
  B lightens
  C cleans
  D sterilizes

15 The source of her income (line 102) is:
  A her savings
  B charity
  C her friends
  D the state

16 Her sister's actions (line 110) after each visit reveal her:
  A rudeness
  B affection
  C fear
  D indifference

17 ONE of the following words (line 120) is incorrect:
  A I
  B didn't
  C have
  D nobody

18 Her doctor (last paragraph) is described as all of these things EXCEPT ONE:
  A large
  B sensible
  C black
  D lively

19 The best word to replace 'extreme' (line 126) is:
  A extraordinary
  B endless
  C final
  D surprising

20 'Tranquillisers' (line 131) are given to patients to:
  A cure them
  B calm them
  C stimulate them
  D reassure them

THE
AMAZING ELEPHANT MAN

When the Elephant Man appeared as if from nowhere in a shop premises in the Whitechapel Road in London towards the end of November, 1884, he was still in the early days of his career as a professional
5 freak. His real name, as his birth certificate bears witness, was Joseph Carey Merrick and his manager was Mr. Tom Norman, a showman who specialised in the display of freaks and novelties.

The shop hired for his exhibition was probably the
10 one then numbered 123 Whitechapel Road. The building has survived until today as one in a terraced row of Victorian shops, though it has since been renumbered as 259. The adjoining premises on the east side then displayed the familiar pawnbroker's
15 emblem of three iron balls high up on the wall. On the west side was the shop of Mr. Michael Greary, fruiterer and greengrocer.

Directly across the road from the row of shops, on the other side of the wide thoroughfare, stands the
20 imposing entrance to the London Hospital. In the 1880's the hospital displayed a long and imposing classical facade, set well back behind railings and with porters'

lodges at the main gates. The whole effect was designed to inspire confidence in the capabilities of medical science, and no doubt a measure of appropriate awe among the inhabitants of the district.

Joseph Merrick was brought here by Tom Norman, both of them hoping that the Elephant Man's impact on London would be a profitable one. Outside the premises, across the shop front, leaving only the doorway clear, the showman hung a large canvas sheet, painted with the startling image of a man halfway through the process of turning into an elephant and announcing that the same could be seen within for the entrance fee of twopence.

A young surgeon from the London Hospital, Mr. Frederick Treves, who visited the freak show, could recall the poster in all its vivid detail when he came to write about it some 40 years later:

'This very crude production depicted a frightful creature that could only have been possible in a nightmare. It was the figure of a man with the characteristics of an elephant. The transfiguration was not far advanced. There was still more of the man than of the beast. This fact – that it was still human – was the most repellent attribute of the creature.

'There was nothing about it of the pitiableness of the misshapen or the deformed, nothing of the grotesqueness of the freak, but merely the loathing insinuation of a man being changed into an animal. Some of the palm trees in the background of the picture suggested a jungle and might have led the imagination to assume that it was in this wild that the perverted object had roamed.'

Whatever it was that could possibly be causing poor Merrick to take on his verisimilitude to an elephant, in displaying him as a freak, Mr. Norman was working in an ancient tradition which could trace its roots far back in the history of fairgrounds and circuses in England. London, in particular, had been noted for its insatiable appetite for monsters ever since at least the days of Elizabeth I.

When Treves arrived outside the shop it was to find the exhibition temporarily closed. Questioning a small boy hanging about on the pavement revealed where the showman might be found, and the lad was persuaded to seek him out, where he was refreshing himself in one of the local taverns. Mr. Tom Norman proved to be unhesitating when it came to striking a bargain: he would open the exhibition for a private view, on condition that the gentleman paid the special entrance fee of one shilling. The scene was set for Frederick Treves's first encounter with Joseph Merrick, the Elephant Man.

Treves was certainly not setting out to write fiction when, towards the end of his life, he finally set down the tale of the Elephant Man for inclusion in what was to be his last published work. His essay, however, is not strictly factual. Above all there is the very curious fact that he consistently saddles Joseph Merrick with the Christian name of John. It is curious, because a whole segment of Treves's life and career came to be intertwined with the destiny of Joseph Merrick, and, as things turned out, it was hardly a superficial relationship.

It seems reasonably certain that it was the door of 123 Whitechapel Road which Mr. Tom Norman, in due course, unlocked and opened, before ushering his visitor from the hospital opposite, into the dark interior. It was difficult for the visitor to pick anything out at first, for the light from the window was obstructed by the large canvas sheet bearing its message to the passers-by in the street. The atmosphere was decidedly cold and damp, and there was a faint but peculiarly unpleasant odour hanging in the air. The main part of the shop was bare and disused, but towards the back a cord had been suspended across the room from one side to another, and what might have been a large red tablecloth hung down from it to form an improvised screen.

As soon as they were in the shop, Tom Norman went across to the screen and drew it aside. There in the half-light beyond, sat the figure of the Elephant Man, seemingly remarkably small in contrast to the impression of something gigantic created by the showman's poster.

He was hunched up upon a stool, and held a brown blanket drawn well up about himself to cover his head and shoulders. The movement of the curtain did not seem to disturb him, for he continued to sit motionless, staring at the blue flame of a gas burner that had been arranged so as to heat a large brick balanced on a tripod before him. This was the only source of heat and light in the room. The very stillness of the almost diminutive figure awoke in Treves the feeling, as he said, that here was the very 'embodiment of loneliness'.

The showman suddenly called out a sharp instruction to the figure: 'Stand up!' Treves says that he spoke 'harshly', 'as if to a dog', implying a certain brutal insensitivity on the part of the Elephant Man's keeper. Yet Mr. Norman was a professional in his own area, and how else would his public expect him to behave when dealing with a creature supposedly half-human, half-beast – a kind of urban Caliban?

But then, as if reluctantly, the Elephant Man stirred and rose awkwardly to his feet, letting the blanket slip to the ground as he turned to face his most exclusive audience. As the covering fell, the souce of the peculiar odour which hung in the air inside the shop became apparent, for the sickening stench, which evidently had its origins in the startling condition of the subject's body, at once intensified.

Treves's medical career had been associated with the London Hospital from the beginning. He had

arrived as a medical student in 1871, become assistant surgeon at the hospital in 1879, and was appointed full surgeon there in 1884. Although he was still only 31, his experience of the appalling range of physical horrors and injuries likely to be admitted into a foundation which existed to minister to the ills of an area which contained some of the worst slums of Europe must have been considerable.

From what he says, however, it is clear that he was shaken by his first glimpse of Joseph Merrick; and perhaps also taken unawares by his revulsion at the sickening stench given off by Merrick's body. He summed up his initial reaction in one memorable phrase: that Merrick seemed to him 'the most disgusting specimen of humanity.' 'At no time,' wrote Treves, 'had I met with such a degraded or perverted version of a human being as this lone figure displayed.'

As he stared, the Elephant Man began to turn slowly about so that his visitor might view him from all angles. The movement re-awakened Treves's clinical instincts, for he noticed how the unfortunate creature showed signs of having at some time in life suffered a disease of the left hip; it had left him lame so that he needed to lean on a stick.

With the return of his habit of scientific detachment, Treves began to make precise clinical observations. Where he had been expecting to see a figure that was both monstrous and large, the Elephant Man was in fact of quite a slight build, perhaps only a little over five foot two inches in height. The upper part of his body was unclothed to the waist, and the lower half was clad in a pair of threadbare trousers that seemed to have 'once belonged to some fat gentleman's dress suit'. The feet were also naked, and his lameness became obvious as he stood there with his body slightly tilted to the left and his back twisted and bent.

Above all, it was the head which created such an amazing impression. this did indeed seem huge beyond Treves's most imaginative expectations: a misshapen mass of bony lumps and cauliflower-like growths of skin. It had the circumference of a man's waist, and the forehead was disfigured by bosses of bony material which vulged forward in great mounds, giving it an appearance something like that of a cottage loaf laid on its side. The greater mound pressed down upon the right eyebrow so that the eye on that side of the skull was almost hidden.

The lower half of the face was itself compressed and distorted by a swelling of the right cheek, where a pink mass of flesh protruded from the mouth, forcing back the lips into inverted folds. Here, then, was the origin of the 'trunk' which the poster artist had so graphically portrayed, if with a certain artistic licence to enhance its resemblance to an elephant's anatomy. There were other bony masses present on the top and side of the skull, but in those areas it was the skin which dominated, the flesh being raised up into heavy cauliflower-textured growths that hung down at the side and back of the head.

Merrick's body itself was in no way spared, for masses of similar pendulous growths of skin hung down from the chest and back. Elsewhere it looked as though the skin was covered by fine warts. The right arm was enormous in size and virtually shapeless, the hand on that side being 'large and clumsy – a fin or paddle rather than a hand.... The thumb had the appearance of a radish, while the fingers might have been thick tuberous roots.'

It was impossible to imagine such a limb being of much use to its owner. By contrast, the left arm and hand looked completely normal, even delicate and feminine in their refinement. The feet, so far as Treves could see, were as shapeless and deformed as the gross right arm.

The showman seemed to Treves to be unable or reluctant to pass on more than the most rudimentary information about his charge: that he was English born, that he was 21 years old and that his name, so Treves understood or later misremembered, was John Merrick.

For his own part, Treves felt a keen perplexity in the face of the malformations which he found himself observing. He was certainly quite unable to account for the condition, to pin on it any label of medical diagnosis or to recall ever having come across anything remotely like it in his professional experience or theoretical training, though Treves was already a figure to be reckoned with in the medical world.

His interest in the case, however, was not concerned with exploring it as medical folk-belief. His mind was quite made up by now that he would like to take Merrick back across the road so that he could examine him at leisure and in detail in his room in the London Hospital's Medical College. Mr. Norman once more proved willing to strike a bargain, for no doubt he saw a publicity value in the idea. It was therefore agreed.

Considerable problems must invariably have been involved in transporting this startling creature about from place to place. The problem, moreover, still existed, even when moving him over a distance of no more than a few hundred yards to the door of the Medical College, which lay along Turner Street, on the south-west side of the London Hospital's main complex of buildings. For the Elephant Man to appear on the streets without concealment was, in fact, to invite the immediate assembling of an unruly crowd.

There was nevertheless a solution to hand – or, at least, a partial solution. It took the form of a special set of outdoor clothes which the Elephant Man could use to conceal himself from head to toe. First there came a pair of huge, bag-like slippers in which the feet and lower legs could be encased. Then there was the voluminous black cloak which practically touched the ground once it was draped round its owner's shoulders.

There remained only the need to ensure the smooth reception of the Elephant Man at the college. So that he might identify himself to the porter and avoid any embarrassing delays at the entrance, Treves handed Merrick his visiting card.

Eventually they stood facing each other, in Treves's room in the Anatomical Department of the Medical School. As the examination and interview proceeded, so Treves became more accustomed to the Elephant Man's distorted and fluting voice and was able to add a little to his background knowledge of the man.

Treves persuaded Mr. Norman to allow his charge to be brought as a case for discussion and diagnosis before the eminent members of a learned medical society, the Pathological Society of London.

Perhaps there was at this point awakened in poor Joseph Merrick's heart, if not the wild hope of a cure, at least the chance of a wise and informed explanation or the assurance that something could be done to halt the advance of his condition. To have allowed himself to be exhibited before a group of medical grandees could, in any case, have been no worse a prospect than exposing himself to the ill-informed curiosity of the majority of freakshow patrons.

After his temporary fame as a medical curiosity, the Elephant Man was forced back on to the road in the early months of winter. There was no explanation offered for his illness, no hint of a possible helpful treatment.

The police closed down the exhibition shop in the Whitechapel Road, responding to the shift in public opinion which was demanding a tightening up on the standards of what should be considered fit for public viewing.

Already, in 1885, the cold draught was being felt in the freakshow business as police and magistrates became steadily more persistent, more determined in their opposition to the exhibition shops.

Joseph was therefore sent on a tour of the Continent, which was a failure, leading him ever more closely to disaster. His Austrian manager finally abandoned him in Brussels in June, 1886, and stole the £50 he had managed to save. Joseph pawned his few possessions to raise enough for the passage home.

To his own consciousness, inside his poor distorted skull, in an advancing state of bewilderment and panic, it must have seemed to Joseph that he was on the road to his final crucifixion. The faces of strangers, who spoke in languages he could not understand, pressed themselves against the carriage windows and gaped in attempts to catch a look beneath the great hat's veilings.

If he descended from the train, the crowd mercilessly followed after his bizarre and shuffling figure whichever way it tried to turn. At Ostend, a blow as savage as any other fell when the captain of the cross-channel ferry, appalled by Joseph's appearance and mindful of the feelings of his passengers, refused to give him passage.

A medical man at Ostend helped him and put him on the way to Antwerp from where he could get the regular, daily packet service to Harwich.

The final stage of his journey began when the train pulled out of Harwich for London. For several days he had been travelling towards a destination that did not really exist beyond the echoing vastness of Liverpool Street station.

When he finally arrived, his will was gone, his demoralisation complete, and the attention which his figure drew to itself was instant, whether he tried to move on or stood stockstill. The crowd gathered with its usual murmuring comments, the fingers pointed, the eyes stared.

It was the police who stepped in and forced back the by now highly excitable crowd, guided the helpless, terrified and extraordinarily top-heavy figure into the haven of the third-class waiting room; then held the doors against the press of people. Joseph at once collapsed into the furthest and darkest corner of the room.

Frederick Treves's morning's work at the hospital can hardly have begun when a message arrived, asking if he would be willing to go to assist the police at Liverpool Street Station. When he arrived, the crowd about the waiting-room was still so thick that the surgeon had some trouble in pushing his way through. As at length he managed to get in at the door and to enter the waiting-room, the figure of the Elephant Man was immediately recognisable to him. It was huddled close against the wall as if trying to shrink away to nothing. Treves realised that his former acquaintance must by now have passed beyond the limits of endurance and be completely broken.

After a few words with the police, the surgeon agreed to take responsibility. With their help he then shepherded or half-carried the staggering Joseph out through a crowd to where a hansom cab was waiting. They huddled him in, and instructions were given to the driver as Treves himself clambered into the confined interior. The Elephant Man questioned nothing, but sat in a silent daze, seemingly all at once overcome with a great, trusting sense of calm. Then, as the cab turned out of the station, he sagged into a sudden and astonishingly child-like sleep.

As they clattered through the streets, Treves, sitting in the cab filled with the well-remembered stench of Joseph's body, must have begun to consider the implications of the responsibility he had accepted.

The righteous system by which society sought to

control the lives of the poor and destitute could offer Joseph nothing to meet his true needs. At best they might shut him away in the anonymous harshness and squalor of an institution to wait his death and so erase himself from the world's consciousness.

Frederick Treves's mind was already made up that the time had come for the rules somehow to be broken, and he was prepared to use his own prestige to that end. Having descended in his hansom cab like a *deus ex machina* to rescue a broken life, he intended to see the role through to the end.

The hansom cab, with its incongruous pair of passengers, returned to the London Hospital, and Joseph was helped to a small single-bedded isolation ward, tucked away up in the attics. Here he was washed, given food, put to bed, and for the moment left to sleep and dream.

There was only one disruption to his new-found peace and quiet when a nurse bringing food, and not forewarned over what to expect, came through the doorway and saw the figure of Joseph for the first time. The tray that she was carrying crashed with its contents to the floor as the woman screamed and ran off down the corridor. But Joseph, propped up exhausted against his pillows, seemed too weak to notice the commotion.

Six months later, an appeal by Mr. F. C. Carr Gomm, the chairman of the London Hospital management committee was launched in the Times for funds to help the Elephant Man. By November, 1886, the blind eye of the authorities could not be relied on to remain turned for much longer. It was obvious that little further improvement could be expected from the treatment the hospital had to offer. He was, moreover, occupying a private ward, urgently needed for other patients and for which no payment was being received.

A vigorous publicity campaign was set off on his behalf. Carr Gomm explained in his letter to the Times: 'He has the greatest horror of the workhouse, nor is it possible, indeed, to send him to any place where he could ensure privacy, since his appearance is such that all shrink from him.'

He made the point that he ought not to be taking up space in an already overcrowded general hospital 'where he is occupying a private ward and being treated with the greatest kindness – he says he has never before known in his life what quiet and rest were.'

The outcome to the Times letter was astounding, and letters continued to arrive by every post. Contributions were sent and a Mr. Singer offered a yearly sum to keep him at the hospital. He had suddenly caught the imagination of the British public in a way that could not have been possible while he remained a grotesque, disturbing showpiece in the freakshops.

Only six months before, it had seemed impossible to visualise any future for him, beyond the inevitability of his being drawn down into Victorian England's insatiable and nameless maw for the destitute and broken in spirit. He also had the advantage of being the perfect object for philanthropic attention; utterly blameless and hence unqualifiedly deserving.

He had entered into his refuge.

Michael Howell and Peter Ford.

THE AMAZING ELEPHANT MAN FOR DISCUSSION OR WRITING

1 'London, in particular, had been noted for its insatiable appetite for monsters ever since at least the days of Elizabeth I' (line 60). Do you think that in the 20th century this appetite has been quenched or are people still fascinated by 'freaks'?

2 Would you have paid to see the Elephant Man? Give reasons for your answer.

3 Do you agree with the form of censorship which, in 1885, opposed freakshows and exhibitions? Who were the magistrates and police trying to protect?

4 Using the information given in lines 290–330, and writing as Joseph Merrick, give an account of your nightmarish journey from Brussels to London.

5 Extracts from a letter Carr Gomm wrote to the Times to rally support for Merrick are given (lines 398–401 and lines 404–407). Write a letter to the paper in which you make a plea for Merrick and request contributions to ensure that his future will be guaranteed so that he need never go 'on tour' again.

6 In the past it was by mounting campaigns through newspapers that one 'caught the imagination of the British public'. How would one attempt to do this nowadays?

7 Treves depicted Merrick as the 'embodiment of loneliness' (line 116). How would you describe him?

FAIRGROUND
PEOPLE

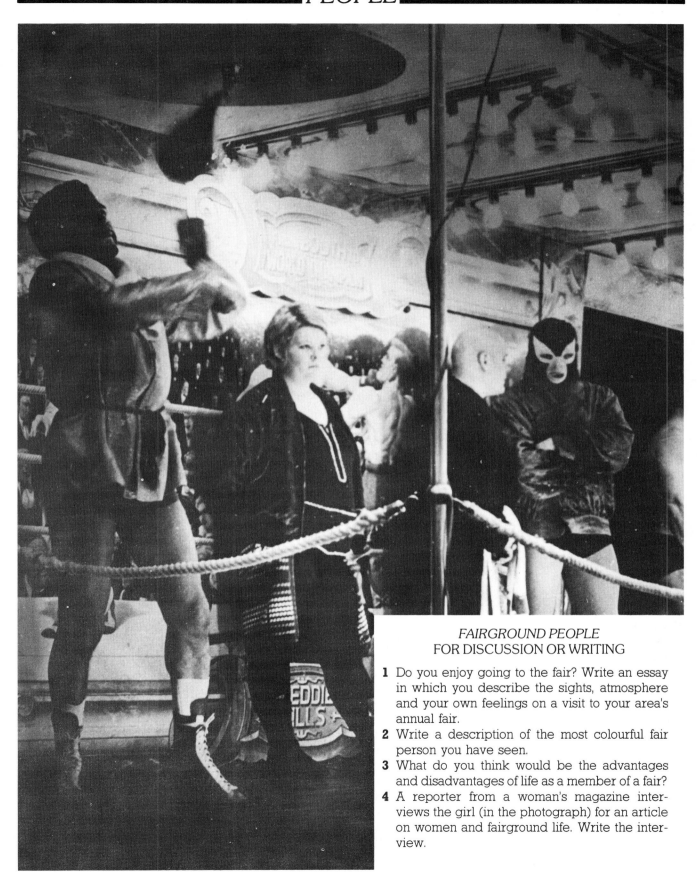

FAIRGROUND PEOPLE
FOR DISCUSSION OR WRITING

1 Do you enjoy going to the fair? Write an essay in which you describe the sights, atmosphere and your own feelings on a visit to your area's annual fair.

2 Write a description of the most colourful fair person you have seen.

3 What do you think would be the advantages and disadvantages of life as a member of a fair?

4 A reporter from a woman's magazine interviews the girl (in the photograph) for an article on women and fairground life. Write the interview.

MAGGIE

I started to go deaf fifteen years ago. In the beginning my hearing loss was slight but looking back it seems as if the feeling of disability was far greater then than now, for it seemed to permeate my whole being. At eighteen, I was a lively, extrovert, intelligent and attractive drama student with very definite ideas about my future life plan which centred largely on a career in the theatre. I found I missed bits of conversation sometimes in noisy situations but this happened so infrequently that I attributed it to lapses in concentration and the Glaswegian accents around me. Little threatening thoughts that I might be inheriting the family deafness were dismissed until the college began to notice my difficulty and I was sent to an ear, nose and throat specialist. He diagnosed hereditary, incurable, progressive nerve deafness and said that I would probably be profoundly deaf in about five years' time. My first feelings were ones of enormous guilt at having 'let my parents down' and I kept the news secret until the college wrote to them. But the guilt of being less than a perfect person remained and grew, as my deafness progressed.

I readjusted my life plan as one who has been told she has five years left to live. I found I could bluff my way out of awkward situations by acting the part of a rather scatty dolly bird. It wasn't true that I couldn't hear you but rather that I was such a feather-brained, aspiring actress that I just didn't understand what you meant. It seemed more acceptable to be a 'normal' silly butterfly than an intelligent deaf woman. In this role I made no demands on anyone but I experienced a different kind of oppression which led me to my first awareness of sexism and the oppression of women in general.

When I thought about a future when I would be profoundly deaf I shuddered with horror. I wouldn't be able to act because I would lose control of my voice. All my present voice training would be wasted. I wouldn't be able to work at anything other than cleaning or assembly line work. I would have to give up my present social life and take up interests where I didn't have to mix with people. I could, of course, get married and take the easy way out of the employment problem. If I were a wife and mother I wouldn't lose my self-respect as it is fine for mothers to stay at home. But would any man want a deaf woman for a wife? Since my deafness was hereditary would I want to watch children of mine go through all this trauma? Would I wish a miserable deaf woman on any child for a mother? Whichever way I turned to think, the negative answer that I was deaf seemed to destroy any shred of hope. I can only think that I learned to expect so little from my future because I had somehow soaked up these prevailing attitudes towards women with disabilities as a hearing woman and taken them over to crush myself in my own deafness.

Five years later, I was married to a life-long friend and working as a teacher of drama in a comprehensive school. The frivolous butterfly had long since vanished into oblivion. I could still hear, with the help of an expensive hearing-aid, and could communicate with my husband and friends quite easily in one-to-one situations. In groups, such as the staffroom at school or gatherings in my own home, however, I was lost, since, by now, I had to see the speaker's face to lipread as well as hear. People's heads toss and turn, mouths are covered by hands, so many consonants look alike on the lips and by the time you have translated one difficult word the next sentence has passed by unnoticed. I discovered that neither hearing-aids nor lipreading were the miracle solutions they were cracked up to be.

Being a woman made things 'easy' once again. I smiled and nodded my way through hour after hour, looked good and cooked nice food. In those days it seemed acceptable for the men to do all the talking and the woman to listen and play the part of passive admiring wives. My armchair interest in the growing women's movement told me otherwise but I couldn't see any way out; I could still ape 'normality' but the woman inside was in despair.

I seemed to be near breaking point when one evening something happened that proved to be the beginnings of my birth as a deaf woman. I was in an Indian restaurant with friends doing my smiling and nodding act when I noticed the people opposite. At first, I thought they were drama students because they were so lively and expressive but then I noticed the sign language. They were deaf like me. They were happy. They were laughing and talking and didn't give a damn that the whole place knew they were deaf. I stared and stared with fascination and found I could follow more of their conversation than I could the talk at my own table even though I couldn't follow the signs. My years of pretence seemed suddenly absurd. I had been making things 'normal' and easy for everyone except myself. I was a deaf woman, it was time to give up my mourning and come out deaf.

As my first positive thoughts about my disability began to take hold I realised that I had been allowing my deafness to deprive us of so much. This body had a right to carry a baby and give birth. In saying our children shouldn't be born I was saying implicitly that I shouldn't have been born. OK so maybe our children could go deaf but with me as a mother they would have

Ron Aldridge and the deaf actress Elizabeth Quinn, in the award winning play 'Children of a Lesser God.'

105 the finest possible expert to help them. Even if they didn't go deaf they were going to have a magnificent deaf mother. Not for our children the passive smiling noddy or the pretty cook. They were going to grow up seeing deaf people treated with respect. It became my 110 most important goal not only for my children but for myself and all deaf people.

Whilst I was expecting my first child I met some women who had been born deaf who introduced me to the most revolutionary hearing-aid ever invented – 115 sign language. Lipreading the clearest speaker is fine for half an hour but after that my eyes water and my brain becomes confused and I am no longer alert enough to continue. No relationship can be made or continued in half-hour stretches but if people can 120 fingerspell or sign I can enjoy their company into the early hours of the morning without strain. It takes ten minutes to learn the fingerspelling alphabet and when people fingerspell the first letters of words I can lip-read them with ease. I find that, once finger-spelling 125 has been mastered and a relationship established, people are more motivated to learn how to sign. There is something very special about communicating with deaf people which can terrify you or enthrall you

depending on what kind of person you are. We look at 130 each other when we talk and this looking plus more explicit non-verbal communication involves a high level of self-disclosure which is not normally present in spoken conversation where people hardly look at each other at all. Words can lie and cover up but the face 135 and body rarely do. My special needs demand your honesty and glimpses of your preciously guarded inner self. 'I'm sorry, don't worry, never mind, dear,' you say when I tell you I am deaf. But it is your face that reads 'fear', not mine.

140 A recent visitor laughingly remarked, 'Your children speak to people as if everyone were deaf.' Yes, they do when I am there because they acknowledge my right to be included – my right to exist. Even when I am one deaf woman among a hundred who can hear it is 145 still my right. When I walk into the busy staffroom at college or join a room full of friends and see them switch, as if by reflex action, to speaking and signing so that I can understand, I feel a glow of joy. This is how it should be because I am important and lovable enough 150 to be included and when I am included I am no longer disabled.

MAGGIE

FOR DISCUSSION OR WRITING

1 Can you explain why Maggie originally felt that 'it seemed more acceptable to be a "normal" silly butterfly than an intelligent deaf woman' (line 29)? Why is 'normal' inside inverted commas?

2 How does Maggie answer the questions she poses for herself in lines 45–50? Do you agree with her answers?

3 'Communicating with deaf people . . . can terrify you or enthrall you depending on what kind of person you are.' Which way do you think you would react? Have you ever had any experience of meeting a deaf person?

4 Write, what you imagine, would be Maggie's diary entries from the time she first experienced problems at College up to the day after she receives her doctor's confirmation that she had 'hereditary, incurable, progressive nerve deafness'.

SUMMARY

A magazine written by deaf people to help newly diagnosed deaf people, has approached Maggie for her story. In no more than 300 words write the article in which she describes her fears, the problems she faced and how she dealt with them.

MERRY

I began to think about how much of the language used about us (who are disabled) is negative. Youngsters would look at me and ask, 'What's WRONG with that lady's leg?' and parents (if they didn't shut the child
5 up and rush away guiltily) would reply, 'She's got a BAD leg.' Not, anyway, the most instructive answer. People talk of us as invalids – in-valid. Well no one was ever going to call me that again and get away with it. Slowly I realised what had happened to me; how I had
10 been condescended to and treated according to people's stereotypes about what I ought to be like; how my leg had so often been politely ignored. I began to see how much energy had to be spent on preventing people from making me look as normal as possible (i.e.
15 as able-bodied as possible). Even more slowly I began to see how, all my life, I had worked hard at being 'well-adjusted' and making sure that that was how others saw me. And it started to become clear what that meant. It meant smiling when I was in pain and re-
20 assuring whoever I was with. It meant only discussing my leg if I could find something funny to tell about it. It meant accepting whatever the doctors did to me (psychologically as well as physically) with unquestioning courage. All in all it meant being very untrue to
25 myself.

Then suddenly the system's role became clear too. I saw that WE are an oppressed group, like people who are black, women and so on; that segregated and substandard education, a physical environment that does
30 not take our needs into account, job discrimination, housing discrimination, lack of aids and services and the threat or actuality of institutionalisation keep us dependent and always ready to please. To justify this treatment, people are taught, through the media for
35 example, to view us in certain rigid and negative ways – as stupid, unable to look after ourselves, uninterested in the world and so on, and so on.

Anyway, now I laugh when I remember how I used to walk faster if I saw another person on crutches,
40 trying to prove I wasn't as feeble as they were. That's the in-group competitiveness that oppression breeds, just like women trying to be more attractive than the others.

So where am I now? Well, I'm in all sorts of exciting
45 and tingly places. For a start I'm doing what I can to change the system that relegated us to dependency. To that end I've joined the Liberation Network of People with Disabilities. We've still got a lot to learn, but we've already got a lot to offer and a lot to teach.
50 Over the last few months I've made lots of close friends with people who are disabled and know a friendship with them quite unlike my friendships with the able-bodied. Some of the other women who've written pieces for this book are people I love dearly and share
55 with so much. We understand a great deal without need for words. We can be human with each other about things that the able-bodied are usually too impatient to wait for or too bound up in only one way of experiencing things to appreciate. We laugh help-
60 lessly together, cry together and are highly committed to each other. We know that when we are fighting to get things right for everyone in our oppressed group, we are fighting for each other, and when we are fighting for each other, we are fighting for everyone.
65 We know we have a whole lot of treasures to offer the world and are happy to know that we still have a lot to learn.

ANGIE

From the age of six years old I attended a residential
school for disabled children. The school was very poor
on education, so much so that at the age of sixteen I
was only at the level of a nine-year-old. I used to go
home at weekends and talk to the able-bodied kids
about what they were doing at school. I had never
even heard of some of the subjects they studied. I felt
so ashamed that they knew more than I did and I was a
lot older. I decided to ask my teacher why I did not do
the same things as my friends did at their school. She
told me it was because I was disabled and that there
wasn't much point in educating me to 'O' and 'A' level
as I would never get a job. I told her I was not
prepared to spend my life in a workshop making
baskets. I was going to improve my education and get
a job in open employment no matter how long it took.
Since the age of twelve I had been very bored with
school life and started to become rebellious. I felt frus-
trated and couldn't explain why. Most of the other
children were not very intelligent and this made me
feel very alone. I could not talk to them as friends. I
tried to talk to some of the staff about how I felt, but in
their eyes we were all the same whatever disability we
had. I was told to go and play and stop bothering them.
This was quite common amongst the staff, never
explaining what their ideas meant. One idea which
most of the staff held was explained to me quite clearly.
I was about fourteen years old and had just finished
preparing a salad in the cookery class. The teacher
came over and said, 'What a good job you have made
of that. You would have made someone a good wife.'
'What do you mean, I would have?' I asked. 'Well,' she
replied, 'What I meant to say was if you marry a
disabled man, you would make him a good wife.' The

school had really strange ideas on marriage and the
disabled. They believed that if a disabled person got
married it should be to another disabled person as it
would not be fair on an able-bodied person to burden
them with a handicapped partner. Anyway an able-
bodied person would not fancy a disabled person. I
didn't go along with this idea at all. I knew for a fact that
able-bodied boys fancied me. I had proved that when I
went home for weekends.

Edited by Jo Campling

SOME SCENES FROM SOCIETY

SOME SCENES FROM SOCIETY

The east end of Glasgow is not like London's East End, a fairly well-defined district with its own character and traditions, but a disaster area, a series of contiguous neighbourhoods sharing a common calamity. It is Calton and Camlachie, Bridgeton and Dalmarnock, Shettleston and Tollcross, all of which at one time formed distinct communities, but which are almost communities no longer, nor distinct, but broken lines of buildings crumbling amidst wastelands, like the last lingering teeth in an old man's jaw.

A group visiting the area on behalf of the Duke of Edinburgh's Study Conference last autumn found themselves 'shocked, saddened and disgusted' by their experience. About a quarter of the homes are overcrowded. About half have no hot-water tap, bath or inside toilet. About one man in five is unemployed. Vandalism is rife. Alcoholism is ubiquitous. Arson is becoming a popular pastime. Tuberculosis, the scourge of Glasgow in the past, but almost unknown in recent years, is making a comeback. The infant mortality rate is the highest in Europe.

'The situation is appalling,' said a consultant in a local hospital. 'We simply cannot discharge patients to damp, dirty, derelict houses, especially when they are recovering from a stroke or chest illness.'

In a room in the top storey of a damp, dirty, derelict house in Monteith Row, by Glasgow Green, I met Norman Barclay, who was recently discharged from hospital and seemed ready to return to it. His hands were shaking, he spoke in a breathless wheeze and his conversation was often cut short by a spluttering cough. He is 64 and looks more.

'Och, I'm in a bad way,' he said, 'but you should hae seen me in mah prime.'

He was in the Scots Guards during the war and rolled back his sleeve to show his regimental badges tattooed on his arm. 'Five years in the war in Egypt, in the desert, fighting for a better world, and I end up wi' this.'

His room, as his next-door neighbour said, was a midden. The paint was peeling and the plaster crumbling, there was dirt and dust everywhere, and the damp was climbing the walls and hung in a chilly suspense in the air. His bed was a heap of rags. There were rags on the floor, rags on a chair, rags on the table. There were four other rooms in the flat, each in a similar state of decay, and each of which houses another individual or family, comprising about a dozen people in all. They all used one gas-stove in the hallway, and one putrid broken-down toilet in an upstairs attic. His rent is ten pounds a week.

Monteith Row is nearly a hundred years old. The most dispiriting sights, however, are the post-war estates, the homes which have degenerated into slums within one generation. Barrowfield, Bridgeton, is a small estate of about half a dozen streets. It was built during the housing crisis of the immediate post-war years when economy and speed were all. The houses are of a uniform brown and almost uniform design. There is never a shop or pub to vary the scene. Sub-teenage gangs vandalise the neighbourhood and whole rows of windows are bricked up or boarded up or covered with polythene instead of glass.

A doctor who was called to the bedside of a patient in the neighbourhood came rushing out of her house after ten minutes with a handkerchief to his face. In 20 years of medical practice he had never witnessed such squalor. The woman was too ill to cope with her large family, her husband was nowhere about, and her children were tearing the place apart. (That particular family has since been re-housed.)

Mr. James Clyde, a 31-year old ambulance controller who is head of an east end community action group, said: 'The planners think that it you put in a bad family with the good, the bad get better. It doesn't work that way at all – the good get worse.' It certainly requires more than ordinary determination in such an area to maintain standards. One woman in Barrowfield Street with six children (the oldest is nine, the youngest one) said that she hardly lets them out of the house. 'I'm afraid that they'll get into bad company and be picked up by the polis,' she told me.

Teresa Casey, a teenager, lives with friends in Barrowfield, but always goes to her grandmother in another part of Glasgow at weekends. 'It's the fights, you see. There's the Torch mob at the top of the estate, and the Spurs at the bottom and on a Saturday night all hell's let loose. The polis come when it's a' over, or sit in their pandas and watch.'

The Glasgow police have made immense efforts to close the gap that has always existed between them and the working class areas of the city. They have for some years now been engaged in an active community involvement programme, and teachers, priests, community leaders all agree that any deficiencies in their effort arise out of a manpower shortage. 'They'll tell you there's not enough policing in Barrowfield,' said Mr. Clyde. 'Well, I'll tell you there's not enough policing here in Dalmarnock, and they'll tell you the same in Calton or Tollcross. But they can't be in ten places at once.'

Statistics in themselves tell one little, for as a police superintendent explained, where violence is endemic and people lose faith in the police they no longer even bother to report it, so that an apparent increase in the crime rate could be the result of increased police vigilance.

There is, however, no gainsaying the statistics on employment. In our first day in the east end, which we spent in and around Bridgeton, photographer Colin Jones and I spoke to about 30 people of whom only *one* – a fishmonger – had a job. The rest were either unemployable or unemployed. The first person I encountered, James McLure, 59, a diminutive man with bright little eyes, had been out of work for 43 years and seemed in no particular hurry to get back into it. 'Who'd give me a job at my age?' he said.

There was a time when Glasgow's east end had a rich concentration of skilled workers, foundrymen, mechanics, craftsmen in the building and engineering trades, but as the area declined they were amongst the first to move. Their move in turn hastened the decline.

Alcoholism is another problem. 'It's not worse now than it was before,' said a priest, 'but God, it's bad enough.' The Scottish alcoholic is less bloated than his English counterpart because he lives and dies mainly on spirits. The ordinary drunk is a familiar and accepted figure in the east end, though something like a tone of censure creeps into conversations when it comes to meths drinkers. But there are beings even lower than meths drinkers, the 'lacquer lads' who seek oblivion through hair-spray mixed with lemonade. They can find neither shelter nor sympathy, and perhaps seek none, and one can see them on cold winter evenings crowded round fires which they make out of rubbish on one of the many vacant lots in the area. When the cold becomes insufferable some may cross the river to a refuge run by a Catholic mission. Others crawl into a dark corner and make themselves as comfortable as they can. Four were found dead in the week before we arrived.

One often hears of 'problem families' in the east end, and it would seem that the definition of a problem family is one where the father can't avoid drink and the mother can't avoid pregnancies. There is little hope of being able to reform the former but attempts are being made to change the latter. 'We can't get very far,' said a health visitor, 'because we're up against the church, but they're having fewer children, even in Catholic families.'

Some communal leaders feel that they haven't gone nearly far enough. Mrs. Betty McAllister, head of the Calton Residents' Association, said, 'I've nothing against bairns – I've got one myself – but where there's too many of them around there's trouble.' When she was shown plans for a new housing estate in which about one third of the houses were reserved for large families, she protested, and the whole scheme went back to the drawing board. 'There's no arguing with Betty,' said a planner.

A Glasgow Eastern Area Renewal project (known as GEAR) was launched last year with a budget of £138m, and the planners have been concerned to involve the local inhabitants at every level. To this end an imaginatively appointed centre has been opened on Bridgeton Cross to display the various schemes envisaged and to invite local comment. (The most common yearning seems to be for 'a house wi' front and back doors and mebee a bit o' gairden.') Mr. Clyde, who heads Dalmarnock Action Group, said he and his associates didn't have to wait for GEAR to see what was happening around them, and they set up their group in 1974. Similar committees have sprung up all over the east end which, said a planner, 'often give us headaches, but they also give us hope.'

Something like a grass-roots movement has now emerged, and Mrs. Betty McAllister is perhaps its best known and certainly its most colourful figure. She is a housewife and mother who runs a busy fish-shop with her three sisters and who somehow manages to find time to run friendship clubs and youth clubs and be the gadfly of every planning office in the west of Scotland.

The GEAR scheme covers an area of 4,000 acres (of which 500 are derelict) and immediate plans are in hand for the building of new homes, shops, factories, schools, sports centres. 'Aye,' said a planner, 'but can we provide a new spirit? We can build factories, but we can't force employers into them. We can build homes, but we can't force people to occupy them. The population of the area's about halved in the past six years, and people are still leaving at the rate of seven per cent a year.'

'It's not too late if they'll get on with it,' said Mr. Clyde. 'But there's too much infighting with the Scottish Office pulling this way, and the Strathclyde Region the other, and the Glasgow District Council a third. I can say this much. If they don't do something to save Dalmarnock within the next six months, there'll be nothing left to save.'

Mrs. McAllister was rather more sanguine: 'You see, with all their troubles you've got guid folk here.'

They are certainly resilient folk. There is Mrs. Kilpatrick, an apple-cheeked woman in her seventies who saw Jones and me wading through the mist on an icy December morning and invited us in for a cup of tea. When we had the tea she insisted – over my protestations – on frying us some ham and eggs – 'You need it in this weather, hen.'

She lives in Barrowfield, in a gleaming, well-appointed home with carpets on the floor and pictures on the wall and mementoes from relatives and friends the world over.

'I don't mind it here,' she said, 'but my daughter is afeart to come often. It's her car, you see. They could have your tyres off you while you're still moving.'

On the top floor of a Dalmarnock tenement made

almost inaccessible by vandalism I met Mr. and Mrs.
James McNeil. They have three children aged two, five
and seven. They live in a room and kitchen without a
220 bath or even hot water, but the place was spotless and
its cheerful, and its immaculate appearance somehow
added an extra dimension to the squalor outside. I
asked Mr. McNeil, a skilled building-worker (who
seems to spend much of his free time making his home
225 habitable) why he hadn't moved.

'We did move,' said his wife, 'to one of the new
estates. The house was decent enough, three
bedrooms, running hot and cold water, but it was just
nowhere. You didn't get to know people and the
230 people you got to know didn't want to know. Dalmarnock's a real place.'

'For the time being,' added her husband.

But perhaps the most lingering memory is that of ex-
Guardsman Barclay. I left him sitting on a heap of rags
235 gazing into his television.

'It's nae workin',' he said, 'naethin' in this house is, but
ah've a guid imagination and I can see anything I
fancy.'

Chaim Bermant
THE OBSERVER MAGAZINE

THE PROBLEM THAT DOESN'T GO AWAY
FOR DISCUSSION OR WRITING

1 A group representing the Duke of Edinburgh's Study Conference visited the east end of Glasgow and were appalled by what they saw. What 'shocked, saddened and disgusted' you as you read this article?

2 Of all the problems mentioned which would you find the hardest to bear if you lived here?

3 A community action group are trying to get Norman Barclay rehoused. Write the report, detailing his problems and the reasons why immediate action is necessary, which will be presented to GEAR.

4 One planner wondered if the GEAR scheme could provide a 'new spirit' in the area. How would you describe the present ethos of the inhabitants of Glasgow's east end?

5 Make a list of the terrible problems to be found in this area. Can you suggest any solutions?

THE PROBLEM THAT DOESN'T GO AWAY
MULTIPLE CHOICE

Lines 1–160

1 'Well defined' (line 2) means:
A clearly distinguishable
B prosperous
C refined
D poor

2 The area is a 'disaster area' (line 3) because:
A there are frequent accidents there
B neighbours are a problem
C it lacks distinction
D it has no sense of identity

3 All except ONE of the following occur in the area:
A excessive drinking
B robbery
C poor sanitation
D setting fire to buildings

4 The number of people suffering from tuberculosis is now:
A decreasing
B non-existent
C increasing
D constant

5 'Derelict' (line 24) houses are:
A empty
B ownerless
C in good condition
D collapsed

6 It would seem that Norman Barclay was suffering from ONE of the following:
A a cold
B a chest and lung complaint
C a war wound
D old age

7 'Putrid' (line 50) means:
A out of order
B private
C foul
D old

8 To describe Barrowfield all except ONE of the following are true:
A the houses are monotonous in colour
B there is little variety of style
C public amenities are lacking
D the houses are too small

9 Damage in the neighbourhood is mostly done by:
A secondary school children
B children aged twelve or less
C unemployed youths
D adults

10 The author thinks that if conditions are to be pleasant it requires:
A an unusual amount of effort
B a mixture of people
C full employment
D a conscientious approach

11 The police have problems in this area because of all these factors except ONE:
A lack of local interest
B lack of effort on their own part
C an insufficient number of police officers
D aggressiveness is part of normal life there

12 It is suggested that the figures relating to the amount of violent crime might be due to:
A the increased efficiency of the police
B lack of trust in the police
C an increase in the number of crimes
D a decrease in religious beliefs

13 The figures concerning the number of people out of work are:
A certain
B vague
C doubtful
D unreliable

14 Skilled workers began to move out of the area:
A before the area declined
B once the decline had started
C long after the decline had started
D only recently

15 Scottish drunks, compared to English drunks, are:
A fatter
B the same
C more friendly
D thinner

16 Meths drinkers are viewed:
A more kindly
B less kindly
C with indifference
D with affection

17 The 'lacquer lads' tend to gather:
A on waste land
B in empty houses
C in shelters
D in the streets

18 Their greatest problem is:
A the weather
B food
C greed
D violence

19 The Catholic Church's attitude to Mrs. McAllister's views would tend to be:
A welcoming
B indifferent
C hostile
D variable

20 The result of Mrs McAllister's protest (lines 153–155) was that the whole plan was:
A re-thought
B dropped
C postponed
D completed swiftly

GLASGOW
5 MARCH 1971

With a ragged diamond
of shattered plate-glass
a young man and his girl
are falling backwards into a shop window.
5 *The young man's face*
is bristling with fragments of glass
and the girl's leg has caught
on the broken window
and spurts arterial blood
10 *over her wet-look white coat.*
Their arms are starfished out
braced for impact,
their faces show surprise, shock,

and the beginning of pain.
15 *The two youths who have pushed them*
are about to complete the operation
reaching into the window
to loot what they can smartly.
Their faces show no expression.
20 *It is a sharp clear night*
in Sauchiehall Street.
In the background two drivers
keep their eyes on the road.

Edwin Morgan

HIGH STREET TERROR OF THE SHOPLIFTING GANGS

The group of young girls rifling through the rack of dresses in a Knightsbridge shop appeared, to the shop assistant's practised eye, to be acting suspiciously.

When she approached them to ask if they needed
5 assistance she was knocked to the floor in a hail of kicks and blows that left her bruised and shaken as her assailants fled into the street.

The shop in which the attack took place – a stone's throw from Harrods in the heart of London's most
10 fashionable shopping district – in the past ten weeks has lost £3,000 worth of goods to shoplifters, mainly, it is suspected, to one gang which visits the shop so regularly that staff identify members by nicknames like Bonnie and Clyde.

15 Although the all-female staff are fully aware that the gang members are shoplifting, they are often afraid to approach them because they fear violent retaliation.

'They come in looking for a fight, wearing dresses you know they have stolen from our rails,' says the
20 shop's manageress. 'It's morally wrong to turn a blind eye, but what can you do? Life is more important than clothes.'

Knightsbridge is not alone in experiencing a more ruthless and frequently violent breed of shoplifter. A
25 Home Office report into shoplifting, published last week, notes a 'new and worrying' development of shoplifters blatantly stealing from stores by force and intimidation of staff and customers.

Stores in provincial streets and shopping centres are
30 particularly susceptible to the trend as large numbers of teenagers mill aimlessly through shopping precincts.

Michael Miller, group security officer of Sears Holdings, which controls the Miss Selfridge chain, says in the past twelve months stores in such disparate
35 areas as Nottingham, Manchester and Hemel Hempstead have been troubled by gangs of youthful

shoplifters up to fifty strong, using intimidation and sometimes violence.

'It's an intractable problem,' says Miller. 'We have a
40 young staff, mostly female, who are not equipped to deal with it.'

In common with many large stores, the Sears Group now employs male uniformed security staff, largely, says Miller, 'to give the staff confidence, but also as a
45 necessary deterrent. It is a growing problem, and as unemployment gets worse it grows even more.'

Big London stores are noticeably reluctant to discuss any changing patterns in shoplifting, presumably for fear of alarming customers. Harrods says it has a policy
50 of not discussing any information about customers or staff. And a spokeswoman for Marks and Spencer said it does not keep records of violent incidents relating to shoplifting and is unable to comment. But security officers at Marks and Spencer branches in the London
55 suburbs confirmed that violence has become increasingly common when dealing with shoplifters.

The security officer of one London branch has been assaulted six times by shoplifters, suffering a broken nose and a dislocated jaw in separate incidents. 'It is
60 mostly gangs that are responsible,' he said. 'You cannot go after one shoplifter without knowing the gang will go after you. Often the most you can hope for is to recover the goods and you have to worry about retaliation – people coming back to get you.'

65 British shops lose an estimated £1,000 million in stolen goods each year. According to the Home Office there were more than 242,300 offences of shoplifting in England and Wales in 1982. Stores in Oxford Street alone, Britain's most popular shopping area, lose £50
70 million a year to theft and 'shrinkage' – the euphemism for pilfering by staff. The Metropolitan Police special shoplifter unit, which deals with suspects arrested in

Oxford Street, makes more than 5,000 charges a year.

Harry Shepherd, chairman of the Oxford Street
75 Association, says the use of violence – 'from thumping
to slashing with knives' – is increasing among shoplifters in the area. Oxford Street stores now employ
more than 200 uniformed security guards while the
national expenditure on deterrents for store thefts and
80 violence amounts to some £150 million, with £3 million
to £5 million spent in Oxford Street alone.

'Ultimately it is the public who have to pay for that,'
says Shepherd. 'Shoplifters now are more ruthless,
more prepared to use violence. It is a reflection of the
85 society we live in. But this is all-pervasive, and the
honest shopper is put to great inconvenience. It's a sad
day when you walk through Harrods and see Gucci
cases chained together to prevent theft.'

The Home Office report, which says violent incidents
90 are still 'isolated', states that the only advice it can give
to retailers under attack is to call the police. But it does
suggest that more shops should participate in precau-
tionary 'early-warning' schemes, alerting other
retailers to shoplifters or fraudsters operating in the
95 area.

Mick Brown
THE SUNDAY TIMES

HIGH STREET TERROR OF THE SHOPLIFTING GANGS
FOR DISCUSSION OR WRITING

1 'It's morally wrong to turn a blind eye, but what can you do?' What does the manageress mean by this statement? How does she justify her position? Do you agree with her?
2 What is the new trend in shoplifting, and how does Michael Miller try to account for it? Do you think his judgement is right or can you suggest other possible reasons for the new trend?
3 Have you ever seen someone shoplifting? If you have what was your reaction?

SUMMARY

In not more than 250 words summarise the problems that beset shop traders as outlined in this article.

KNIGHTS OF THE NEW YORK SUBWAY

Every night of the week between 8 p.m. and 4 a.m., unarmed young men and women in red berets and T-shirts that proclaim them to be the Magnificent Thirteen Subway Patrol, ride the noisy, graffiti-covered
5 trains concentrating on the worst routes, the least well-lit stations and the poorest, most violent neighbourhoods. It is a job without financial reward, a mission of danger, a labour of love. And the youngsters who do it are – there's no other word for it – amazing.
10 The patrolling began in February as violence mounted in the subways, producing something close to panic among the public. The New York Subway Transit Authority increased the number of uniformed policemen on patrol, but not before Curtis 'The Rock'
15 Sliwa (pronounced 'Sleever') and his dirty dozen had put on their red berets and descended into the dank underworld to keep the peace. 'When people see us in our colours, clown time is over,' Sliwa says crisply.

Within four months the original 13 grew to almost a
20 hundred and more recruits are joining all the time. They are in their late teens or early 20's, most of them have some training in the martial arts and all are as streetwise as alley cats. Sliwa expects membership to

rise to the thousand mark by the end of the year and
25 when they have made some sense of the subway, he says, they are going to take on Central Park and 'clean it up'.

'Meet us down at our storefront in the Bronx,' says Mr. Sliwa on the telephone, sounding more like the
30 chairman of Chase Manhattan than a poor, 23-year-old Polish-Italian American who graduated in garbage-collecting and street-fighting. The storefront, the group's headquarters, is just off Fordham Road in a decaying section of the Bronx. Fordham Road itself is
35 still a busy commercial artery and forms the dividing line between white and Puerto Rican neighbourhoods. The Magnificent Thirteen's HQ is on the Puerto Rican side wedged between two over-crowded and noisy tenement buildings. The group is tolerated on its tiny
40 patch of turf but not liked.

The shop-office is a clutter of broken chairs, an old typewriter, a filing cabinet, a furled American flag and sundry junk. The group are putting on their red headgear (Boy Scout berets minus the badges) and
45 getting ready to go out on patrol. A fight has broken out up the street but Sliwa and his men ignore it. Only one

---

of them actually lives in this district but two years ago, led by Sliwa, they formed the 'Rock Brigade', a community-oriented group which helped to clean up
50 the garbage and improve the neighbourhood. All of the original 'Thirteen' were members and there is a strong sense of comradeship between them as well as great affection and respect for 'The Rock', their charismatic leader.
55 We set off. A normal patrol is three or four youths per train; the first shift is from 8 p.m. to midnight, the second from midnight to 4 a.m. The Transit Authority police finish at 2 a.m., so until the Magnificent Thirteen got going the dangerous small hours went unpoliced.
60 'When the cops go off at 2 a.m. it's Looneyville,' says Sliwa.

We reach Fordham Road station and prepare to board the No. 4 train on the IPT, the Lexington Avenue Express, which goes from the Bronx via Manhattan to
65 Brooklyn, from battle-zone to battle-zone through one of the richest pieces of real estate on earth. The time is 8.31 p.m. Sliwa and his comrades wait at the turnstile until they hear the train approaching, checking fare-

jumpers and keeping an eye out for potential muggers
70 and victims.

A Transit cop, weighted down with a double belt on which hangs a revolver, several pouches of bullets, radio, keys, night-stick, notepad, handcuffs and torch, stands in the shadows near the entrance. The boys, in
75 stark contrast, carry no arms and rely entirely on their quick wits, street savvy and, what they repeatedly refer to as, their 'presence'. 'The beret and the T-shirt shows the public who we are,' Sliwa explains. 'We've got no arms, the muggers know that. But they also
80 know we aren't going to step backwards.'

8.40 p.m. We board the Lexington Express. A drunk lurches towards Sliwa, hangs on a strap staring at him, no response, lurches off.

8.43 p.m. Train stops at 183rd Street/Jerome Avenue.
85 Another heavily-laden cop gets on. The boys move towards the doors and look down the platform checking for each other's red berets. If one is missing that means trouble and they will race down the train through the interconnecting doors to the scene of
90 action. Three black girls enter, recognise the Magnifi-

cents – they've had quite a lot of local publicity – giggle a bit and ask for autographs. An elderly white man says, yes, the kids are doing a great job. The express train rattles and shakes its way through Manhattan at 95 high speed. To speak and be understood you have to shout.

9.01 p.m. Between Wall Street and Bowling Green the train fills with smoke. The policeman, who has had 13 years riding the subway, confirms that the Magnifi- 100 cents are doing well. 'If I weren't here,' he says, 'there'd be no trouble with these guys around. It's psychological warfare down here and they know how to handle it.'

9.27 p.m. Utica Avenue, Brooklyn. Change trains and 105 go four more stops to Junuis Street/Livonia Avenue. Kato Lee, a 20-year-old Hawaian Chinese, black sash in Kung Fu and martial arts instructor, leans over and marks my subway map with a rectangle over the area we have just entered – Brownsville, Brooklyn. 110 'Muggers' delight,' he says.

Train stops and we get out. Station is dimly lit and apparently deserted. Looking over one side of the elevated platform there is total devastation – Berlin 1945, Belfast, Beirut, Brooklyn, there isn't much dif- 115 ference in that murky light. On the other side human beings live and, as Sliwa says, they have to travel on the subway whether they like it or not. He tells us to check the number of lights in the token booth (equiv- alent to our ticket office) as we pass. We do: seven 120 powerful bulbs, and inside with the token-seller, sits a policeman.

We go down to the street and cross it, watched by a cluster of men hanging out on the corner. They shout a few obscenities but do not move. We climb the steps 125 on the opposite side and walk along a narrow elevated pathway that leads to the next station. There are light sockets but no lights. Water drips, shadows tremble, footfalls make a ghostly sound, conversation dies. A battlefield is a more friendly place.

130 Sliwa stops halfway along. 'Two months ago, Keith and Philip (two of his closest friends, one black, the other Chinese) and me were coming along here about midnight. We smelt the peppermint of angel dust before we saw them. Six guys trying to rape a woman. 135 We went in. One of them, a giant, picks up Keith by the neck, strangling him. I kick him in the head – left my footprint on his face – but it didn't do anything. Philip kicks him in the groin. He doesn't fold up in the normal way, he just goes down flat, out, still holding Keith by 140 the neck. We shout to the woman to run but she's too scared or something. Finally, she begins to move as we're fighting the other guys but then one of them pulls out a sawn-off shotgun from under his coat and points it at her. Another yells: "Kill the bitch, shoot her." He 145 raises the gun and I let fly another kick but I'm off balance. The blow makes the gun go up and hits him in the face. The woman takes off and I go sailing through the wire fence 20 feet down on to the street below. The guys take off and I finish up in hospital, but it's not too 150 bad – just some bruises, cuts and strained muscles.'

At the other station there is another brightly lit token booth and another Transit policeman inside it. The police never patrol the 75 yard walkway that links the two stations for a very good reason – it's too dangerous. 155 Two of the group escort an elderly woman home. She has told them there are some men lurking around the station and is frightened.

10.32 p.m. Sutter Avenue. The underpass, though well lit, reeks of urine, enough to make you gag.

160 On the *LL* train to Broadway Junction, East New York, still in Brooklyn, Kato Lee, who has just formed a new group in the Borough of Queens where he lives and is carrying their berets and T-shirts in a plastic bag, described his technique. 'If there is a guy harass- 165 ing a woman in the train, I go up to her and say, "Is he bothering you?" If she says, "yes", I ask him to stop. If he says "no", then I teach him a lesson.' We are sitting close to Lee at the end of the rear carriage – the most dangerous one at night – and I ask him what would he 170 do if two men were as close as that and began to insult and provoke him.

'Language is no problem,' he replies. 'We train our- selves to stay cool, shrug it off.' But where is the point of no return? 'Put your hands on my leg,' he says. I touch 175 solid muscle. He makes a small horizontal movement with his hand, the cutting edge moving towards my throat. 'Now you're dead,' he says. His other hand makes an identical gesture towards Peter Howe, the photographer. 'And you're dead too.'

180 10.35 p.m. Broadway junction. Sprawling, labyrin- thine interchange where four lines cross. Sliwa points out favourite haunts of muggers waiting for their victims. The boys eat at a fast-food kiosk. Sliwa is taller than all of them and walks with a military stride. He is 185 smartly turned out in neatly-creased brown trousers and black patent leather shoes. He got his nickname from prowess as a street-fighter at high school and his ability to go days without sleep.

He is articulate to the point of despair for the poor 190 scribbling reporter. He is 'multi-lingual' in a city where the rhythms of the English language have such variety and importance. 'I can talk white and I can talk black,' he says. And he is romantic. 'We ride the trains to help take the fear out of the people. We're not a gang, we're 195 all individuals. We don't have warlords, capos or any of that shit.'

10.58 p.m. The A train – 'the quickest way to Harlem' – to Times Square. A rookie cop says you can't take pictures and pulls out a small sheet of regulations to 200 prove it. Somewhat ironic, since we have been taking pictures all evening of policemen in the subway.

The Transit Authority's patrolmen – tripled since the

crime wave – have nothing but good to say for the
young men in the red berets, but the hierarchy is non-
205 committal and a little put out that Sliwa rejected offers
of joint patrols and an integrated communications
system.

11.26 p.m. Times Square. Some of the group go up to
wander around and keep an eye on things in the slea-
210 ziest, raunchiest showpiece of New York. As they
leave, one is struck by their ordinariness. They all
come from working-class backgrounds and are as
racially-mixed as the city they defend, a deliberate
policy, Sliwa says, to show there is no prejudice and
215 that they wish to protect all communities. During the
day they work in places like McDonald's, the A & P
supermarket chain, Treacher's Fish and Chip shops
and a few go to college. During the long nights they
spend their own money on subway fares and snacks.

220 So far there have been no dropouts though some
recruits were rejected. 'A few of them had the wrong
idea,' says Dino Reyes, an Italian-Spanish youth of 18
and the comedian of the group. 'They were either too
prejudiced or too aggressive.'

225 Sliwa stresses that they are not aping Charles
Bronson in the film 'Death Wish'. 'We are *not* vigilantes,'
he says. 'It could be done but vengeance is not our
line. We're out here to protect people, not lynch them.'

12.34 a.m. Walking back to the store-front along the
230 Fordham Road in the Bronx. The front line between
white and Puerto Rican territory is quiet although
groups of men hang around on the street-corners. 'The
Rock' and his number two, Arnaldo Salinas, an 18-year-
old Puerto Rican boxer and street-fighter, stride along
235 confidently, clear targets in their red berets. There is,
however, nothing macho about them which makes
their confidence all the more impressive. Perhaps the
heavies on the street corners also sense this because
no one seems keen to take them on.

240 Sliwa's favourite topic now is Operation Central
Park, an ambitious scheme to make the New York's
equivalent of Hyde Park, St. James's and Green Park
rolled into one, safe again for lovers after the sun goes
down.

245 'In early August,' he says, 'we're going to move in a
hundred of our guys. We'll patrol in threes with some of
them up in the trees. We'll use walkie-talkies, flares
and handcuffs and, of course, our presence. And then
. . .' he grins as he says it, 'all them scallywags will have
250 fear in their hearts.'

John de St. Jorre
OBSERVER MAGAZINE

1 Is there a need for this type of patrolling in
England? If you think there is, identify the
areas and say what the problems are.
2 Why do you think Sliwa and his 'Knights' are
more successful in their efforts to curtail
violence than the police?
3 How does Sliwa differentiate between the
'Knights' and 'Vigilantes'?
4 Would you be willing to give up your nights,
use your own money for tube fares and work in
intensely dangerous territory as a 'Knight'?
Give reasons for your answer.
5 An elderly lady approaches the 'Knights' for
help. Write a vivid account of the incident
either (a) from the woman's viewpoint or (b)
from that of one of the two knights who escort
her home.

COMPREHENSION
Lines 1–80

1 What territories do the Magnificent Thirteen
patrol? (3)
2 How could their work be described? (3)
3 Why did they begin their patrols? (2)
4 What is Sliwa's long-term plan? (1)
5 What did Sliwa and the Magnificent Thirteen
do for the inhabitants of the area where their
office is situated? (2)
6 What do Sliwa and the group members do as
they wait for the train at the turnstile? (2)
7 Sliwa and his comrades are 'in stark contrast'
(line 75) to the Transit Cop. Why? (4)
8 When the train arrives in a station what routine
do the Magnificent Thirteen follow? (3)
9 Give the meaning of the following as used in
the passage:
  dank underworld (line 16) (2)
  artery (line 35) (1)
  charismatic (line 53) (1)
  potential (line 69) (1)

Mr. Speaker, sir, I would like to submit a modest proposal on behalf of some fifteen million of our fellow citizens who did not vote at the last election – and few of whom will do so at the next.

This Citizen's Bill proposes that the government appoint a Minister for Children. (A new minister does not mean setting up a whole new ministry. Jennie Lee was a special minister given a special task – to set up the Open University. She was, if I remember aright, offered something like four civil servants with which to accomplish the mission. It was done.)

What is sought is the short-term appointment of a minister – the missing tribune in this House – who represents *over the period of one or two Parliaments* a possibility of resolving some of the shocking examples of our tattered social policy towards the child that I shall give.

Before I do so, one natural question needs an answer. Children have parents. If they have a minister as well, is this not a blow to the family itself? Not at all. Some children do not have parents, or have become wards of the state. Some actually *ask* to be taken into care, like the sixteen-year-old daughter of an English mother and a Pakistani father who wants to go to a sixth-form college, but has been told she will be sent to Pakistan for an arranged marriage. The magistrate, following the book, refused the request made on her behalf by the Social Services Department. The answer must be to change the book.

Presumably that is what the House had in mind in setting up a select committee to enquire into why children were in care, and under what conditions they were growing up. Often, one suspects, not under the conditions in which your boy or my girl is being reared. The select committee is asking why some eight-year-olds are being locked up, like multi-murderers, in high security and sometimes solitary confinement. Social workers have been asking that question for twenty years. Parliament has been deaf – because there has been nobody to represent those children.

Other children have to be protected from the family. The last Parliament saw the introduction of a Bill which made it illegal for a child to travel in the death seat of a car. It is estimated that this will save the life of a child every week of the year. It took the lottery of a Private Member's Bill to achieve this.

Select committees, by themselves are no guarantee of results. The Select Committee on Violence accepted that 300 children were murdered by their parents every year in Britain, and a further 3,000 gravely injured. That is almost one child killed every day, and ten savagely attacked. The committee's report gathers dust on the shelf.

Nor is there much the family alone can do to prevent their baby from dying or being born mentally or physically handicapped. Parliament set up the Social Services Committee enquiry into perinatal and neonatal mortality. That came to a conclusion which everyone in the medical profession has been expressing for years: that of the nine thousand to ten thousand such babies who die each year 'one third to one half of the deaths are preventable, if modern knowledge and care were universally applied. This amounts to at least three thousand to five thousand avoidable baby deaths each year'. Three years have gone by since that report was filed. Presumably up to fifteen thousand lives have been needlessly lost. Further, 'the number of children surviving each year with important handicaps that could have been prevented is probably at least five thousand'.

These deaths and failures are *not* primarily the responsibility of the family. They are *not* resolved by a Private Member's Bill or a select committee, however helpful those might be. No policy for the family – by itself, and however welcome – can meet many of the most urgent cries for help. I could add many other examples.

Among those which are all too clear has been the snail-like progress towards child-proof containers for medicines. It was shocking to hear a minister actually boast of having passed minor legislation over screw-tops (often optional) which might have saved hundreds of young lives. He seemed to expect a pat on the head. But the United States has had much stronger legislation for over a decade. Is it that Mr. Marconi is having difficulty getting his signals across the Atlantic? Or is it that the pharmaceutical giants resent the extra cost that saves an emergency call (sixteen thousand children rushed to hospital last year) or life itself (twenty-five children die annually)?

I would like to table three questions, other than these, that such a minister might list on his first morning in office.

One. Why do we still have so many children in prison? Child imprisonment was supposedly abandoned in 1908. Yet it still takes place in the most extraordinary forms. Sometimes babies and toddlers go to prison with their mothers, or are born and partially reared there. I have seen such children at Holloway, Askham Grange in Yorkshire, and the closed women's prison at Styal in Cheshire. Their conditions are utterly unsatisfactory; no one in this House would remotely dream of their own sons or daughters being treated like this. None of these babies have committed any criminal offence or appeared before judge and jury. Their numbers are not large, some twenty or thirty at a time; but the very idea of even one being brought up in prison – dogs, barbed wire, flashlights, sudden checks – would inspire not horror, but incredulity in any other Common Market country.

We have recently managed to secure an assurance that girls under sixteen will not be sent to a women's prison. But boys have no such protection, and since the conviction rate for juvenile offenders is just under seven thousand a year, it is clear that a vast amount more needs to be done (after the farce of 'the short, sharp shock') first to prevent teenage crime, and then to treat offenders in a way which is *less* likely rather than *more* likely to stimulate them to repeat and escalate their behaviour.

Two. Why do we have no policy at all for children under five? The DHSS is responsible for day nurseries, playgroups, childminders. The DES is responsible for nursery schools and infant classes for the 'rising fives' (civil service jargon for elderly four-year-olds). The DHSS has spent more than thirty years steadily closing down day nurseries until they are now emergency-only centres. The DES has spent the same years scraping in whatever funds it could to expand towards nursery education for all. Did they never talk to each other? Almost a million children under five have a working mother. What sense does this make to them?

Three. Why can't we have real education for parent-hood in schools? Boys and girls have babies within months of leaving the classroom and we complain that they are often ignorant and unprepared. Yet we have had them in compulsory education for eleven years. We may have told them all about quadratic equations and mediaeval three-field systems but where has been the time to learn about feelings, relationships, future marriage and children?

So the agenda is formidable. Schools, prisons, housing, roads, hospitals; parents, police, social workers, teachers, volunteers, neighbours. The place, rights and responsibilities of that non-voting fifteen million erupts all across our landscape. This was tragically seen in the enquiry into the death of Maria Colwell. She or her family were visited by the teacher, the police, the social worker, the doctor and by all the fragmented agencies that affect the child. In miniature, her case reflected the parliamentary haze, disunity and happenchance in planning for the child. She was seen in professional segments. Only the neighbours saw her as a whole child.

Mr. Speaker, I move that someone in government takes special responsibility for the voiceless fifteen million. And that that person be a Minister for Children.
Brian Jackson
SUNDAY TIMES

A VOICE FOR THE YOUNG
FOR DISCUSSION OR WRITING

1 Do you feel that there is a definite need for a Minister for Children? Why?
2 Of the general observations Brian Jackson makes about the fate of certain children in Britain which surprised you the most? Give reasons for your answer.
3 Brian Jackson tables three questions. Take each in turn and say (a) whether you agree with his point of view and (b) what solution to the problem you would offer.
4 Are there any points, important to you, that you feel he has neglected? What is your grievance and what changes would you like to happen?
5 In the eyes of the law a child becomes an adult at the age of seventeen. Do you accept this limit or would you raise or lower that age?
6 Very often, when it is a question of money, children have to pay the adult rate. Has this happened to you? Give examples of this anomaly.

OLLY: THE SHORT LIFE AND TRAGIC DEATH OF AN EX-PUNK ROCKER

At 4.15 p.m. on Saturday, February 19, the station sergeant at Maidstone police station made a routine check of cell number one into which 21 year-old Oliver Clairmonte had been placed an hour earlier. He found him hanging by his red underpants from a bracket on a water pipe leading to the lavatory in the cell.

Oliver had killed himself in a most distressing way little over an hour after being involved in an affray with security men at a local shopping centre. During his arrest, the inquest heard last week, he had head-butted a policeman.

It was not his first time in a cell. He had hit a police-man once before and been sent to detention centre for three months on one of William Whitelaw's 'short, sharp shock' sentences for youngsters. When he came out he vowed to his father that he would kill himself rather than spend another night in a police cell.

On March 2, his funeral took place at Vintner's Park Crematorium, Maidstone. It was attended by those who loved him, punk rockers and old ladies alike. Cyril Lee, a family friend, addressing the sobbing young-sters, for whom the toughest exterior was no bar to grief: 'For a young man just 21 to feel that there is nothing more to live for, for him to bring his life to an end, means that we, who have something to live for, have failed him . . . if only we never again allow anyone to feel so very deeply distressed, so alone and so hurt, so rejected'.

One mourner unable to be at the funeral was Rat, who describes himself as Olly's 'best living friend'. In the beginning there were four friends in Brighton who saw themselves romantically as the four musketeers: Olly, Irish Adrian, Rat and Poser. Now there are only two: Olly and Irish Adrian are dead.

Adrian killed himself shortly before Christmas jumping off a building. 'He might have been doing it for the crack, thinking he'd walk away from it,' said a friend last week.

Oliver's death confuses both friends and family. But Rat, at least, understands suicide. He talked in an untidy bedsitter in back-street Brighton about how it feels to be young, unemployed, with no money and, in some senses, no hope.

'We're not punks,' said Rat, who has earnest blue eyes and soft non-spiky mohican hair. 'We're rock-and-roll suicides. We've all been into so much glue, drugs, drink and enjoying ourselves that in the end it's suicide, whether by accident or on purpose.

'I know I'm not going to survive another three years, not necessarily because I don't want to but because I'm the kind of person who goes way over the top. If I have to take drugs, I want to take as much as possible.

'I've had a laugh in my own way – and when I die I'll go in my own way, not on purpose, but because everything is just too much.

'When you see kids die, hang themselves, then your friends die . . . when someone like Olly goes like that, it puts the fear of Christ up you . . . you think you are beating the system, taking drugs and getting out of it, and not getting nicked, but in the end you can't beat it completely.'

Johnny Cramp, another friend, sat on the floor in T-shirt, cardigan, dark trousers and brown brogues, his tangerine candy-floss hair the only bizarre feature about him. 'To see friends die really hits you. It makes me determined to live. But I know I'm dying. My liver has gone. My ambition was to be a rock-and-roll star with £500-a-day habit, but I seem to have started at the wrong end of it,' he said wryly.

'I feel old and tired, We're all dying you know, but not Olly. He was a survivor, not like us. He could take speed for six months and give it up, just like that. The other day I took the stereo to bits, unscrewed it all and laid it out bit by bit because everything was so black: I don't suppose I'll ever get it together again.'

While Oliver's friends mourn in their own peculiar fashion, his father, Christopher Clairmonte, an artist who lives in Brighton, lightly fingers a card. In deepest

sympathy. A single rose, and inside a two-line note 'from someone who disapproved of everything Olly did – but who says all that needs to be said.'

He sits at a small table, the walls of the drawing room covered with drawings and paintings of his own. On the floor is a large green frog looking remarkably like one of the trophies Olly might have found on a gnome-pinching expedition with Rat.

'Olly is dead and I am consumed with guilt,' says his

father. 'He became involved in this tremendously powerful, nihilistic sub-culture in which they give the impression of helplessness on the one hand and extraordinary antagonism on the other.

'He was a very charming, pleasant sort of human being who would be extremely nice to old ladies – he once staggered his step-grandmother both by his ability to eat spaghetti and deliver compliments. He looked up from under his rainbow-coloured hair and said, "What lovely bright eyes you have" – and yet at the same time his appearance terrified old ladies into crossing the street.

'The punk life was so much more attractive than the straight life. They live for the day, thinking they are in some ways superior to us as though they know something we don't. They are curiously arrogant about their elders and at the same time astonishingly naïve. They don't imagine I ever screw the wife – or that we've been adolescent as well.'

Oliver's parents' marriage broke up when he was 11 – and his father, after consulting friends who had been children of divorced parents, decided he would not 'play Father Christmas' at weekends.

'The whole thing is a great cock-up and a private tragedy. As a child Olly was uncomplicated and sunny natured, everything you could wish for in an 11-year-old. He couldn't wait to leave school and he always had rather good jobs in which he quickly got promotion – and yet there was always this pull of the schizophrenic life, wanting approval on one hand and saying "I don't care" on the other.

'He had skated on thin ice for the last four years and if I had a phone call saying he had been sentenced to six years' imprisonment, it wouldn't have surprised me.

'Oliver had a case history and a half, a string of motorbike offences which didn't look good on paper, but until he hit a policeman on Bank Holiday three years ago, he was just a naughty boy. I had offered to give him the money to be anywhere else but Brighton that weekend, because he was such an obvious target and leader for the police.

'He was challenged by his friends to shave off his mohican and become a skinhead like them. He did it that morning. He'd been a skinhead for a day when he thumped a policeman.'

Olly had a sense of humour. Once, when told to get a new suit and tie for a court appearance, he returned with a tailcoat and diamonte dog collar.

'When he came out of detention centre, he was confused, very anxious and nervous of the police – and then he discovered glue. I can see hundreds of Olivers standing outside hamburger bars, killing time, displaying themselves and posing, fuelled by cheap drugs and easy girls – but what do you do as a parent? You can't lock them up.'

At the time of his death Oliver had long dark hair and none of the flamboyant insignia which marked him out so clearly among the Brighton punks. He had returned to Maidstone where his mother, Sheila George lives.

He had found a girlfriend, Faith, and moved in with her and her two children whom he called 'the little monkeys'.

'I don't think I'll ever be able to work out why he did it,' said his mother. 'Although I did not approve of some of his actions we never failed to have a good relationship. I never liked him as a skinhead but he knew, and wore a woolly hat. He was concerned about how he looked – perhaps for that reason he put his trousers back on before committing suicide.'

What drove Oliver Clairmonte to his death? Was he keeping his promise to his father that he'd sooner die than face another night in detention? Was it the desperate action of a young man terrified of being in circumstances beyond his control? Or, as Rat suggests when looking ahead to his death, the inevitable result when everything in life is 'too much'?

Mrs. George said, 'His death hasn't hit me yet. Oliver was an ingenuous boy of great charm who didn't see life for himself as a grey-faced commuter. He had had lots of girlfriends but, ironically, he seemed recently to have got close to Faith and her two children and for the first time was considering responsibility other than for himself.'

Alison Miller
THE SUNDAY TIMES

> ### OLLY
> ### FOR DISCUSSION OR WRITING
> 1 Does this story reflect a cultural or a generation gap, or both?
> 2 What do you know about 'short, sharp sentences' for young offenders? Do you think this is the right way to deal with offenders like Oliver? If you do not, what would you suggest?
> 3 Has society failed people like Oliver or is Oliver, alone, responsible for his death?
> 4 Are you sympathetic towards Rat and Johnny? Give reasons for your answer.
> 5 'Olly is dead and I am consumed with guilt,' says his father. Do you feel he is to blame? What steps would, or could, you have taken, if you were Oliver's father or mother, before his arrest in Brighton?
> 6 Do you agree with any of the theories put forward in the second to last paragraph as to why Oliver committed suicide? Have you any other suggestions to offer?
> 7 There are many trends in young society: punks, skin-heads, mods, teds etc. Choose one such 'fashion' and try to explain why young people are drawn to it.

'On the rampage again ... the travelling louts of football' was the headline over one account of the incident that had resulted in Allan spending a weekend ('fifteen to a cell, a good laugh it was') in
5 police cells in the West Country and earned him his second conviction.

It had happened at a service station on the motorway after West Ham had won away in January. Allan had hitched a ride home on the coach carrying the West
10 Ham 'firm' at the centre of what turned out to be a pitched battle, but he had made his own way to the game, Inter City 'on Persil. They got this special offer,' he explains. 'Been goin' this season an' they was goin' last season as well. You send 'em these silly tokens off
15 the washing powder an' get cheap vouchers for train travel. Buy one, get one free, right?

'I just sent off for another five. That means 15 tokens. But what I done was, I saved three tokens then just made it look good by putting 12 bits of cardboard in
20 between. You usually put a false name in case you get into trouble. Last one I filled in I put down "Ronnie Biggs".'

Allan is 19 and lives on a council estate close to the northern outskirts of London. It is a small estate, made
25 up of low-rise blocks that act as a buffer between tidy mock-Tudor semis and a monotonous light-industrial sprawl.

Hampshire Court has been vandalised to the extent that one block, recently vacated, has had toilet bowls
30 and sinks heaved out through the windows. But it is not a battleground, it's just dead.

Allan moved into the Wembley area when his parents did because he had to; he was still at school. The attractions were a better job for his father, who is
35 with the Post Office, and a better flat. The block they'd been living in, in Paddington, was a dustbin anyway, so they left with no regrets. Allan was born in the Roman Road, near West Ham's ground in the East End. And it is to the East End, where they only know him as
40 'Wembley', that he returns most Saturdays during the season, and midweek when there's a game on.

It doesn't matter that it takes the best part of three hours, by Tube, to get there and back. Any more than it does that all his wages, when he's earning, and everything he can scrape together when he's not, go on following West Ham up and down the country. Allan has made the headlines many times in his capacity as a 'Hammers' supporter, or what Fleet Street calls variously, a 'thug', 'maniac' or 'hooligan'. He used to have his own cuttings library in which these words featured heavily in dense, smudgy print. But it was accommodated in a handsome wallet ('twenty-four quid new, real leather') that he'd 'half-inched' from Debenham's and which was itself lifted from his back pocket at last season's Watford game.

He's started again though, and fully expects the following day's West Ham–Chelsea Derby to bring new additions to the collection. As a 'ruck', it shows all the signs of being a monster.

> *Boot boys! – home or away*
> *Boot boys! – don't care what day*
> *Boot boys! – at a match or a pub*
> *Boot boys! – they never give up!*
> *BARNEY AND THE RUBBLES*

Allan was initiated into the rites of Upton Park when he was 12, by cousins older than himself. They were skinheads, obsessed with how many eyelets there were in their 'Dr. Martens' boots and how short they could crop their hair and, although never a 'skin', he quickly built up a name for himself as a bit of a hard-case at school.

'I don't want to sound big-headed but I had a bit of a reputation,' he says. 'I was definitely a bit naughty, yeh.' He was smoking heavily by the time he was 12, and going with his parents across to the pub. 'Me an' the old man used to drink 'Pils' four or five years ago,' he says matter-of-factly,' before it got well-known.'

Not alone among the 16-year-olds jamming the Job Centres, Allan had originally had his eye on the music business as a career, and persistence got him the start he was looking for. Working as a despatch clerk at £25 a week, however, was hardly the go-go world he'd been led to expect, and so he left to take up the electrical apprenticeship from which he would eventually be fired for 'cheeking-up' the foreman.

From being an apprentice electrician, Allan went on to become an apprentice machine-fitter, which he was until he was made redundant last November. Losing his job, however, coincided with losing the girlfriend he'd met in Spain in the summer. And at the same time, his father, who had been separated from his wife for some time, was forced out of work through ill-health. Cooped up in the flat together all day, they got on each other's nerves so much that Allan's father, who didn't like him bringing the 'animals' who were his friends home, ended up putting him out on the street. The result of all this was a two-week stay in what Allan's friends still don't realise was a psychiatric hospital. He

had been about to throw himself under a lorry.

'That will remain with me for the rest of my life, I reckon. It's the worst sort of feeling,' he says, 'I've ever had in the world, y'know. I used to break down in the bedroom an' all that. Me old man didn't have a clue what was goin' on. I didn't give a f— about anything. But goin' in with a load of gerries... There was a woman in there an' her husband an' her daughter came to see her quite a lot, but she never used to eat or nothing. She looked so cut up inside, I don't know why. But the others were just sort of simple. A bit slow, nothing to worry about, know what I mean?'

These are the sort of thoughts that, caught on his own, Allan will volunteer without prompting.

In preparation for what experience has taught him will be the main excitement of the day, Allan as usual is wearing nothing that might get him noticed: shiny-topped Hush Puppies, jeans, neatly parted retro-Mod hair, and a black Melton jacket with an L-shaped nick below the shoulder. (The nick above his left eye, inflicted by 'some nigger' the last time West Ham played Luton, has left an oblique, raised scar.) He's wearing no claret-and-blue because he's not a 'Christmas tree'.

Last season, the South Bank at Upton Park, was partitioned by metal railings, and one side, the left-hand side, behind the goal designated for visiting supporters only. The result is that this south-west corner has become a well-defined battleground that the 'Hammers' hard-nuts feel must be endlessly infiltrated and 'taken'.

'If there's a team coming down with a reputation, you might gain there. It's difficult, 'specially if they're from the North, 'cause the Old Bill's got it well sussed now. But against a team like 'the Yids' (Tottenham), say, or Chelsea,' Allan says as he saunters towards the gate, 'you *got* to. You got to put a showing on at home. It's prestige, like. You can't let other supporters walk all over you.

'I mean, before, Chelsea have really been battered at West Ham. Massacred on the terraces, that's all you can call it really.'

Which explains, perhaps, why the visitors' enclosure is a sea of bilious, pinched faces and limbs that will not stop fluttering. But the Chelsea supporters are not the only ones with a bad case of the shivers: Gary, a print worker, who has travelled from North-West London with Allan, is undulating like his own image in a fun-fair mirror, and several times seems on the point of fainting. Allan, however, hands in both pockets, head back, seems to have been overtaken by a peculiar calm that lights his face and draws the skin tighter. It is how he will look on the night of July 3, some months later, as he presses on, against all advice that it is a no-go area, up Uxbridge Road, in the direction of the Hambrough Tavern in Southall to see the soon-to-be-notorious '4-Skins'. The riot he finds himself in the thick

155 of will add a new dimension to his cuttings library.

For now, though, he threads his way into the centre of the South Bank, directing discreet nods at the many unidentified West Ham supporters occupying the Chelsea 'end'.

160 There is never any question of if it will happen, only when. And when it does, it happens fast and is signalled by a small boy's terrified wailing.

The visiting manager – 'A big hand for one of yesterday's heroes, ladies and gentlemen, Geoff Hurst' – has 165 just completed his first inspection of the pitch when the long anticipated 'ruck' erupts in the middle of the South Bank.

It is the cue for supporters in the West Stand to let loose with lethally sharpened coins and half-full cans, 170 and to immediate effect: blood starts to spring out of mouths and eyes as freely as the sense of panic and exhilaration that rifles through the crowd. The West Stand turns as one to face the Chelsea enclosure with Nazi salutes, while from all parts of the ground the cry 175 goes up of 'Kill, Kill'. From the carnage it could be the scene of a natural disaster.

Allan and his crew escape the police by making a run for it at the last minute up on to the pitch and down into the south-east corner, to regroup, 'It's so well 180 sussed out now,' he says, 'it's just like organised crime.' Later, in Robin's pie-and-mash in Queen's Market, it is deemed to be not, after all, one of the memorable 'rucks', but it sparks off reminiscences of others that were.

185 'Remember that time a couple of season ago, I think we was playing Leicester,' Allan says, 'an' there was a big steam in the South Bank, all these Leicester supporters getting kicked to f—. All the coppers were runnin' round not knowing what to do, but there was 190 this one copper, right, an' he had a West Ham badge on, on his uniform, just inside. An' he's goin': "Go on, lads, kill the bastards!" Ah, it was bleeding magic when he said that.'

When West Ham won the F.A. Cup in 1980, for the 195 supporters who live on the satellite estates in North London and out in Harlow, Thamesmead and the other New Towns, it was as if a way of life they'd heard about, but never experienced, had been fleetingly resuscitated. 'Everybody was singing, everybody was 200 talkin' to each other, all the doors was open an' there was parties all the way up the Barking Road. Beautiful it was,' Allan said with feeling, 'Really beautiful.'

A smash of glass and the rumble of boots –
An electric train and a ripped up phone booth –
205 *Paint spattered walls and the cry of a tomcat –*
Lights going out and a kick in the balls –
that's entertainment
Days of speed and slow time Mondays –
Pissing down with rain on a boring Wednesday –
210 *Watching the news and not eating your tea –*
A freezing cold flat and damp on the walls –
that's entertainment.

THE JAM

There's a poster of The Jam on his wall in Hampshire 215 Court. Allan reckons The Jam.
'There's a lotta truth in there, I tellya,' he says, his finger on the fast-forward button, cueing another track.

Gordon Bunn
SUNDAY TIMES MAGAZINE

PORTRAIT OF A FOOTBALL HOOLIGAN
FOR DISCUSSION OR WRITING

1 Can you explain why Allan, obviously a fanatical football supporter, enjoys and takes part in the violence that erupts at matches?
2 Allan likes the 'The Jam' and 'Barney and the Rubbles'. From the extracts of their songs given in the article how do the lyrics and Allan's thoughts coincide?
3 Is there any way to prevent the 'rucks' which occur so frequently at football matches?
4 Have you ever witnessed violence at or on the way to a match? Write a description of what happened and what your reaction was.

JONES AVOIDS HORROR INJURY AFTER ATTACK BY DERBY COIN THUGS

The Derby terraces are facing closure following a coin attack on Chelsea's Joey Jones.

And the Wales defender revealed to me: 'If it had landed half an inch lower, it would have taken my eye 5 out.'

The Jones incident went almost unnoticed, buried by the disgraceful ripping up and hurling of seats by irate Chelsea hooligans incensed by Saturday's 2–1 FA Cup defeat.

10 The coin left Jones with bruising above his eye and a stitch in a head wound that bled profusely.

Laughing

He told me: 'It was the Derby fans who were responsible and I don't know why. They were even laughing at me.

'Kevin Hales was injured and I went over to see how he was with the referee close by. The next thing was I got hit by these coins.

'Luckily there is only a scratch, surrounded by bruising. I needed a stitch in my head as well.'

Derby face at least as stiff a punishment as Leeds, who had their terracing closed between games after Kevin Keegan was pelted by a coin at Elland Road a couple of months ago.

This is a more serious incident because Jones received injuries. However, the Welsh international stressed: 'I don't want to see their ground closed – I just want to forget about it as quickly as possible.'

Great Yarmouth referee Alf Grey, in his report to the FA, will describe the coin throwing. Grey, in his 23rd and final season as an official, said: 'Derby fans were throwing coins during the match and one hit Jones above the eye.

'A bit lower, and he would have lost the eye. There is no question it came from the Derby section of the terraces.

'One of my linesmen was repeatedly spat upon from the same section of the crowd.

'Jones, to his credit, did not make a great issue of the incident.

'All the players deserve credit for avoiding incidents that could have incited crowd reaction – they were tremendous.'

Chelsea chairman Ken Bates pledged last night that there would be no serious crowd repercussions next Saturday when Derby go to Stamford Bridge for a potential powder-keg situation.

But Bates said: 'Chelsea are better organised to handle big crowds. No disrespect to Derby but it is a provincial town.'

If there is any trouble at Stamford Bridge involving Derby fans, chairman Mike Watterson has threatened to quit.

FA chairman Bert Millichip is demanding an all-out war against the soccer thugs. He said: 'It's time we forgot the freedom of the individuals and started arresting the hooligan leaders. They are the ones we must get hold of.'

Ian Gibb
SUNSPORT EXCLUSIVE

BELT UP, BATES

Ken Bates is the chairman of Chelsea Football Club – an office that, this morning, ranks among the more dubious of sporting distinctions.

For, contrary to what Mr. Bates might think in more emotional moments of delusion, he leads a club that is followed by a bunch of criminals who are destroying our national game.

The Chelsea scum have a record of sickening violence stretching back well beyond his short association with a once-great club.

Hit

And they lived up to their appalling reputation again at the weekend wrecking part of Derby's Baseball Ground just as their counterparts from Leeds had done a week earlier.

Yet, in apportioning the blame, Bates paid special attention to, would you believe, the Press!

'You got what you have been waiting for,' he told assembled newsmen in what must go down as one of the most outrageous Press conferences of all time.

'Newspapers write for their readers and have contributed to this violence. The match received the biggest build-up since Joe Bugner's title fight.'

There are occasions when the most talkative of men would be better advised to belt up. This is one of them.

The insinuation of this particular chairman, still relatively wet behind the ears, is that newspaper anticipation of trouble from Chelsea fans helped cause it.

Frankly, Chelsea's record of violence is such that, far from warning them or fining them, the authorities would be entitled to . . . *kick them out of the League.*

Newspapers do not gloss over trouble in our sporting arenas.

We reflect public concern and campaign for public safety. We are hell-bent on ridding the game of louts like those who follow Bates' Chelsea.

If he thinks otherwise he's burying his head or attempting to deflect responsibility that lies at his feet and those of fellow chairmen.

John Sadler
THE SUN

JONES AVOIDS INJURY AND BELT UP BATES FOR DISCUSSION OR WRITING

1 If the authorities did decide on the closure of the Derby terraces following the Jones incident do you think this is adequate, too light or too heavy a punishment?

2 Do you think that the actions of the players on the field influence crowd behaviour?

3 John Sadler, in his article, is obviously furious with the Chairman of Chelsea Football Club for his remarks following the Derby–Chelsea match. Who do you think is right?

4 Do you agree with Sadler that the responsibility 'lies at (Bates') feet and those of fellow chairmen'? If you do not agree, where would you place the responsibility?

I ask myself, what is it about it? And I'm not the only one, you know. Many people feel like me. But I can't keep going, not when you hear all the things they're saying to you every day. Then, you know, two people will have a fight and it will never end, and everybody round it is a part of it. If you want one person to win and you tell this to the wrong person then you lose some more friends. It keeps going like this too. It's not only black against white, but mostly that's what it is. That seems to be all that's happening in school these days. You can't tell the teachers about it. Of course they know, but if you tell them, the other kids think you're weak, or scared, or not loyal to them. No one is allowed to tell anybody they're afraid. I tell my best friend, Jessie, but I wouldn't tell anybody else. Some days I get so scared before I have to go to school I feel like I'm going to, you know, throw up. I run into the bathroom but nothing happens. I know it won't because it's nerves.

Every day I walk by this long brick wall. You have to go through this little passage way to get to school. There's usually a cat there climbing around. When I see him I tell him, 'Bring me good luck.' He usually runs away which I tell myself is a good sign. Then I tell myself, 'No matter what anybody tells you, don't be upset, don't be afraid.' Sometimes it works, but most of the time it doesn't, especially if Jessie isn't with me. It's better when she's with me. I'd rather have someone yell out, 'There goes two nigger girls', than have me be there all by myself. You don't know what they're going to do next when they do it, and it's always happening. You don't know what's the best thing to do either. Like they'll say, 'Hey, you short nigger, what are you, some kind of a pygmy?' That's my own special name because I'm short. Aren't they clever! I never know what to do.

Some people say, 'You shout back at them so they won't do it again.' But I couldn't get myself to do that. What am I supposed to do when it happens, like, when we're on the playground or the stairs? Or in the class too? It happens in class too. 'Hey pygmy, you read the lesson for today? What am I supposed to do? Jessie says I should keep my mouth shut and tell one of the boys, like, the biggest person I see, 'That kid over there called me a pygmy.' That's what she says to do because she says if we don't start fighting back they'll never stop doing it to us. Maybe she's right, but I can't see myself going up to some guy and telling him what someone said to me.

The boys tell us too, to tell them. They say they'll go after anyone we want them to, that they're not afraid of a single person in the school. I can't believe what's going on. If you tell someone, you don't know what kind of trouble you may be starting, and if you keep your mouth shut, you know what you're letting go on. But everyone keeps saying, 'They aren't going to hurt you, nothing will happen.' But I don't see why they should be allowed to call me things that has to do with my being coloured, and that's mostly what they yell. Everybody fights about it. Even Jessie's been in some fights. I didn't see her, but I did see another a few months ago. I got so frightened *that* time I did throw up. One of the worst things was what I was thinking about, how, like, at first I was afraid she would get hurt and I started to cry, and then, without even thinking about it, I found myself hoping she would kill this white girl. I was crying but I wanted her to kill the white girl. I think mostly because the girl was white and because of what she said. She called Jessie some horrible name, I didn't even understand it at first. Jessie didn't either, but you could tell it wasn't a compliment.

Then, you know, when they fight, everybody crowds round and then they start fighting, like they did this one time when Jessie fought this girl Shea. They were all fighting, and I ran away because I got scared. That time I told my mother, which I usually don't do. My mother told me she was going to school to see what was happening. She went too, but the master told her there was nothing the school could do if children fought before or after school; it wasn't their responsibility. He didn't think the fighting was all that bad. 'Kids have always fought,' that's what he told my mother. He said he was surprised she would find all this new. Didn't she have fights in her neighbourhood where she went to school? That's what he told her. I mean, that's what I know he told her, because some of the other things she wouldn't tell me, but she told my father. I know one of them was that I was supposed to be known as a little bit of a baby, that's what the master said; that just because I was a girl didn't mean I shouldn't have to fight and protect myself. He said he thought coloured people were teaching this to their children. She said she thought he was prejudiced, and he told her our kind are too sensitive about all this stuff. Besides he said, he did a special favour for us letting me into the school when we moved here because he could have said no because the classes were so big. My mother told him no one in this country does any favours for us and he told her she was wrong; that's all coloured people do is ask for favours. Anyway, he said there's nothing that could be done about the fighting. It was happening in the school, sure, maybe once a week too, which is a lie because it happens all the time, but the problem isn't the school, it's the country. So my mother said, 'You mean it's all *our* fault', and he said, 'You said it, Mrs. Davies, I didn't.'

I was surprised too, because I thought the master

was a real nice man. At least *I* never saw him do anything bad to anybody. I don't know all that much what the other kids think of him. Jessie hates him because he blamed her that one time for starting the fighting which she didn't. I know, because I was there. But I always thought he liked us. Like, Mrs. Brainaird likes us. She's always asking me how I'm doing and if I have problems. I don't talk to her, but maybe I could. You can't tell with some of these people, like, how they're going to be if they have to take a side. I think a lot of the teachers would like to take our side once in a while, but they're afraid what the master or the assistants might say to them. Lots of them aren't much better off than we are, I guess, although they don't talk about it with us. Well that's not completely true, because Mrs. Strandy, she told Jessie and this other girl how she was afraid to teach in the school with all the fighting, so she was looking for a new job. They had a long talk about it. Jessie told her maybe she could do something to make it better, but she said, no, she was leaving, even if it meant she wouldn't be able to find another job. She'd rather go on the dole than teach here. That's what she said. Then she told them, it was better before they let all the coloureds in. Can you believe her saying this to Jessie, who's coloured! She didn't even realise what she was saying. She told them, it was better before they let the coloureds in. So Jessie said, 'Well, Mrs. Strandy, if you haven't noticed yet, *we're* coloured.' So Mrs. Strandy said, 'Of course I know you're coloured, but it's not the children I'm talking about it's their parents! It's all your fathers who don't work and don't want to, and all your mothers having all these children. That's what the matter is. It's never the children's fault.' So Jessie just looks at her and says, 'Oh!' That's all, just oh!

Doesn't my school sound like a wonderful place? Now do you know why I don't like going around there, no matter how much I might learn, which I don't think is all that much. Most of the time all I learn is that a lot of people in my school think I'm a coloured pygmy, but I ought to be learning a little more than that. And another thing, if these people, like the master and Mrs. Strandy, have all these feelings about us, I would like to know how they can be allowed to stay in the school, and some of those people have the most important jobs over there, you know. They make the decisions and they have all these ideas. That's all we hear from them: it's the coloureds. Pretty soon, it will get bad for me and I really will be able to throw up before I walk to school, instead of just thinking that I do. Like, right now, telling all of this to you gives me the same feelings I have before I walk there in the morning. It's like I need my lucky black and white cat to tell you what I *think* about school, and we aren't anywhere near school now, are we? I'm not sure where we are here, but it feels that we're a long, long way from school. At least I hope it's a long way from school. I know this isn't really a holiday but I'm trying to pretend it is.

Polly Davies, interviewed in hospital. from:
GIRLS ARE POWERFUL
edited by Susan Hemmings

TO SCHOOL WITH FEAR
FOR DISCUSSION OR WRITING
1 Do you sympathise with Polly or not? Give reasons for your answer.
2 Have you ever been frightened to go to school? Write an essay 'To School with Fear' in which you show why and what your feelings were.
3 Do you think that Jessie's belief that 'if we don't start fighting back they'll never stop doing it to us' is right, or can you suggest another answer to the problem?
4 In the conversation between the master and Polly's mother, whose point of view would you support or do you think that each has a strong case?
5 Do you think that the National Front and the British Movement should be banned by the Secretary of State? Give arguments for and against such a move.
6 Is there any way to improve social relations in this country? Can education help to eradicate the problem?

ON THE NEW BEAT IN BRIXTON

PC William Fearnside-Speed knocks on the door of one of the black clubs on the Front Line, focus of the bitter 1981 riots in Brixton. The door opens a crack and is slammed in his face.

But then it's opened again by another man who asks cautiously what he wants. 'We want to take you up on your kind offer of a cup of tea,' says the PC carefully.

'You want West Indian tea, China tea, or what?'

'Ordinary Indian tea will do.'

'We got no Indians here, man.' Laughter breaks some ice, and the two constables are shown into the kitchen. Reggae with ganja fumes drifts in from other

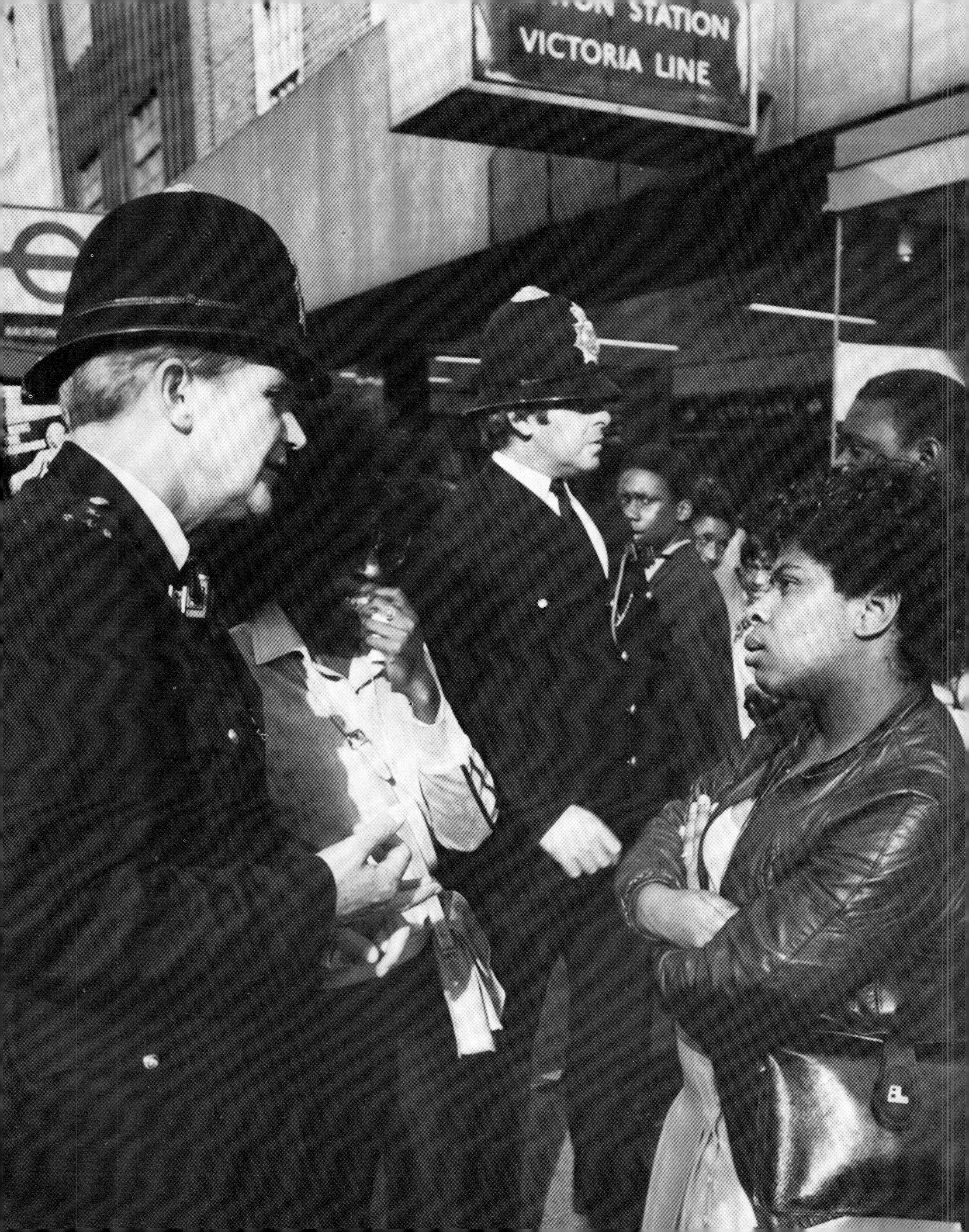
STATION
VICTORIA LINE

rooms, and several young men put their heads curiously through the door while the PCs hold their helmets and sip.

'Some of you coppers are all right,' says one. 'But some of you are bent. Some of your mates fitted me up once.'

'Prove it,' says PC Fearnside-Speed, a little prickly.

'Prove it?' yells the young man. 'I was let out of Borstal after two weeks – it was in all the papers.'

'What papers? What date?' persists the policeman. The rumbustious lady cooking rice and peas interrupts with her more relaxed views of police-black relations, ending with an alarming imitation of Instant Response Unit officers piling out of their van.

PCs Fearnside-Speed and Jonathan Smith are part of a team of 21 sergeants and constables putting in some dogged and intensive legwork round the Front Line, which has become a public symbol of difficulties between the police and Britain's black people.

The work tends to be repetitive and unexciting, and they stand an excellent chance of getting their faces punched in. But their efforts are, according to the local police, producing some remarkable changes in the atmosphere and the crime pattern.

'My correspondence and feedback shows the area is now largely law-abiding,' says Chief Superintendent Bob Marsh, head of Brixton police station. 'People feel that they can not only drive but walk confidently round that area, and local residents suffer much less from noise and nuisance.'

In the station canteen, Fearnside-Speed and Smith are cheerfully abused by PC Philip Stock, another member of the two-month-old Front Line patrol team. 'A fat lot of good you two are when the aggro breaks out,' he says.

It turns out his partner was attacked, called a 'shit' and left lying on the ground with a split lip by an angry man smelling strongly of drink. Both the PCs' radios failed to work, and the attacker 'legged it'.

Didn't this kind of thing tempt them to treat all black men as potential police-bashers? 'The first guy who thumped me when I started work at Brixton was a white man,' says PC Stock wryly. 'The colour of the person who thumps you doesn't really matter – the important thing is to avoid being thumped. My mate won't take out a duff radio again in a hurry.'

As well as making themselves known and being pleasant to people, the patrols have instructions to tighten up on law-breaking. Some obvious inconsistencies arise – such as taking no action in a club where cannabis is smoked, while frequently arresting people for possession in the streets nearby.

The officers are using the same basic methods – intensive stop and search on 'reasonable suspicion' – as the officers in Operation Swamp, the secret and now infamous anti-robbery drive which is popularly believed to have sparked off the first round of riots.

But this time it's winter, with fewer people on the streets anyway; the officers are there constantly, not mounting a sudden invasion; and the community-police consultative group, set up on Lord Scarman's recommendation, was told in advance what was to happen – albeit in something of a rush.

Out on the ground again, a friendly local mechanic strolls over to talk to Clive Noblett, a sergeant at 24. He complains that an officer on the other side of the road recently stopped him about his car tax; the sergeant interrupts with a cheerful lecture about how this might mean invalid insurance and the like.

Finally, though, the man's point is understood: the tax disc couldn't be seen from where the officer was, and he suspects the main reason he was stopped was because he's black. Another man comes up and asks him angrily: 'You squealing on the lads again?'

So far there has been one person stopped and questioned every 11 hours in an area containing little more than a dozen streets, with about 80 per cent of the suspects being black. Up to January 11, the 728 stops resulted in 280 arrests, 161 for drug offences and the next most common categories drunkenness and offensive weapons. It sounds like a doubtful crusade against petty crime, with cannabis smokers elevated to public enemy number one. What about the most worrying local crimes – robbery and burglary?

'You mustn't make the mistake of separating the two,' says Mr. March. 'Drugs is a criminal activity. The big dealers use the local lads, who can then get into other things. The places where dealing goes on can be safe havens for other people operating outside the law. This kind of operation can't expect to catch the big robbers and burglars, but it helps to keep that kind of people away.'

There is a parallel CID operation going on to 'target' robbers and burglars and big-time drugs dealers through intelligence and surveillance – the police had a camera position in a high tower overlooking the front line until recently. The targeting has produced 52 arrests in 28 days.

There have now been several complete days without a single robbery reported in Brixton, which is remarkable.

Another patrol, PCs Duncan Redpath and John McDonald, hear their numbers coming up on the radio, which sends them round to a pool hall where a handbag has been stolen. The angry owner pledges terrible mutilations if the culprit is found. A two-year-old girl who saw the theft points out three passing black men, and the PCs set off rather doubtfully after them.

The three are angry to be stopped, but agree to

come back; the owner says it was none of them. They disappear noisily without hearing the officers' thanks for co-operating.

There are, as Sergeant Noblett remarks, not many perks on the Front Line patrol. Every so often officers are diverted to a stint in the area cars, answering 999 calls, to give them some variety. But if the hopes of the senior officers are realised, some important bridges are taking shape.

'A lot will depend on the manner of the stop and the officer's attitude,' says Mr. Marsh. 'It does him tremendous good to make a mistake and have to apologise. There's no harm in humbling himself on occasions; some people will always resent being stopped, but the intention is to make the area a better place to live.'

Stephen Cook
THE GUARDIAN

ON THE NEW BEAT IN BRIXTON
FOR DISCUSSION OR WRITING

1 This passage shows how the police have tried to achieve better relationships between themselves and the people in Brixton, following the 1981 riots. Do you think that this community policing is a good idea? Should this type of patrolling be done in other areas which have had problems? Would community policing in all areas with a high crime rate be effective?

2 Have you ever been stopped and questioned? Explain what happened.

SEEING THE ERROR OF THEIR WAYS

The pass rate among Asian-trained doctors taking an important Royal College exam has virtually doubled since a small problem of transcultural encounters was identified.

The problem arouses suspicions and counter-suspicions of insult, oriental shiftiness, anger and indifference. It centres around different traditions of eye-to eye contact and it is to be emphasised at a special conference on cultural differences next month.

Examiners at the Royal College of General Practitioners have already been told that it is perfectly good behaviour for Asian candidates for membership of the college to look away from them during interviews. Asian students are to be advised that they can without disrespect look a British examiner or patient straight in the eyes.

'Our people are taught from childhood that to keep looking into the eyes of a person you respect is a great insult,' said Dr. Bashir Qureshi, a member of the education committee of the college's north and west London faculty, which is organising the conference.

The letters MRCGP after a name are an important career qualification for a general practitioner. But Dr. Qureshi, a GP in Hayes, said that until this year the un-officially announced pass rate among Asian candidates was an unacceptably low 5 to 8 per cent a year. 'This was incorrectly claimed to be racial prejudice,' he added.

In the May and June examinations, after the cultural difference had been explained to examiners for the first time, the pass rate rose to 15–18 per cent. 'It was a direct result of educating the examiners,' Dr. Qureshi said.

John Ezard,
THE GUARDIAN

SEEING THE ERROR OF THEIR WAYS
FOR DISCUSSION OR WRITING

1 Asian and Western people have different behavioural customs during a conversation. Explain what these differences are and say how you think they can lead to needless difficulties when 'East' and 'West' talk together.

2 Have you ever been on holiday within the British Isles and been surprised by the behaviour of the locals? If so, how has it differed from that of people at 'home'?

M *(I was sitting on my bed, smoking. Caliban on his usual chair by the iron door, the fan was going outside).* What do you think about the H-bomb?

C Nothing much.

5 **M** You must think something.

C Hope it doesn't drop on you. Or on me.

M I realise you've never lived with people who take things seriously, and discuss seriously. *(He put on his hurt face.)* Now let's try again. What do you think

10 about the H-bomb?

C If I said anything serious, you wouldn't take it serious. *(I stared at him till he had to go on.)* It's obvious. You can't do anything. It's here to stay.

M You don't care what happens to the world?

15 **C** What'd it matter if I did?

M Oh, God.

C We don't have any say in things.

M Look, if there are enough of us who believe the bomb is wicked and that a decent nation could

20 never think of having it, whatever the circum-stances, then the government would have to do something. Wouldn't it?

C Some hope, if you ask me.

M How do you think Christianity started? Or anything

25 else? With a little group of people who didn't give up hope.

C What would happen if the Russians come, then? *(Clever point, he thinks.)*

M If it's a choice between dropping bombs on them or

30 having them here as our conquerors – then the second, every time.

C *(check and mate).* That's pacifism.

M Of course it is, you great lump. Do you know I've walked all the way from Aldermaston to London?

35 Do you know I've given up hours and hours of my time to distribute leaflets and address envelopes and argue with miserable people like you who don't believe anything? Who really deserve the bomb on them?

40 **C** That doesn't prove anything.

M It's despair at the lack of *(I'm cheating, I didn't say all these things but I'm going to write what I want to say as well as what I did)* feeling of love, of reason in the world. It's despair that anyone can even con-
45 template the idea of dropping a bomb or ordering that it should be dropped. It's despair that so few of us care. It's despair that there's so much brutality and callousness in the world. It's despair that perfectly normal young men can be made vicious and
50 evil because they've won a lot of money...

C I know your lot. You think the whole blooming world's all arranged so as everything ought to be your way.

M Don't be so wet.

55 **C** I was a private in the army. You can't tell me. My lot just do what they're told *(he was really quite worked up – for him)* and better look out if they don't.

M You haven't caught up with yourself. You're rich
60 now. You've got *nothing* to be hurt about.

C Money doesn't make all that difference.

M Nobody can order you about any more.

C You don't understand me at all.

M Oh, yes I do. I know you're not a teddy. But deep
65 down you feel like one. You hate being an underdog, you hate not being able to express yourself properly. They go and smash things, you sit and sulk. You say, I won't help the world. I won't do the smallest good thing for humanity. I'll just think of
70 myself and humanity can go and stew for all I care. *(It's like continually slapping someone across the face – almost a wince.)* What use do you think money is unless it's used? Do you understand what I'm talking about?

75 **C** Yes.

M Well?

C Oh ... you're right. As always.

M Are you being sarcastic again?

C You're like my Aunt Annie. She's always going on
80 about the way people behave nowadays. Not caring and all that.

M You seem to think it right to be wrong.

C Do you want your tea?

M *(Superhuman effort).* Look, for the sake of argument,
85 we'll say that however much good you tried to do in society, in fact you'd never do any good. That's ridiculous, but never mind. There's still yourself. I don't think the Campaign for Nuclear Disarmament has much chance of actually affecting the government.
90 It's one of the first things you have to face up to. But we do it to keep our self-respect, to show to ourselves, each one to himself or herself, that we care. And to let other people, all the lazy, sulky, hopeless ones like you, know that someone cares. We're
95 trying to shame you into thinking about it, about acting. *(Silence – I shouted).* Say something!

C I know it's evil.

M Do something, then! *(He gawped at me as if I'd told him to swim the Atlantic.)* Look, a friend of mine
100 went on a march to an American air-station in Essex. You know? They were stopped outside the gate, of course, and after a time the sergeant on guard came out and spoke to them and they began an argument and it got very heated because this
105 sergeant thought that the Americans were like knights of old rescuing a damsel in distress. That the H-bombers were absolutely necessary – and so on. Gradually as they were arguing they began to realise that they rather liked the American.
110 because he felt very strongly, and honestly, about his views. It wasn't only my friend. They all agreed about it afterwards. The only thing that really matters is feeling and living what you believe – so long as it's something more than belief in your own
115 comfort. My friend said he was nearer to that American sergeant than to all the grinning idiots who watched them march past on the way. It's like football. Two sides may each want to beat the other, they may even hate each other as sides, but if
120 someone came and told them football is stupid and not worth playing or caring about, then they'd feel together. It's *feeling* that matters. Can't you see?

C I thought we were talking about the H-bomb.

M Go away. You exhaust me. You're like a sea of
125 cotton wool.

THE COLLECTOR
FOR DISCUSSION OR WRITING

1 The Campaign for Nuclear Disarmament is still very active in England. Do you agree with M. that the C.N.D. does not have 'much chance of actually affecting the Government'? Is her stance preferable to C's who says, 'You can't do anything. It's here to stay' and is happy to sit back and do nothing about it? What would you do?

2 How can the ordinary people of a country persuade their government to listen to their wishes.

3 Would you go on a protest march? Give reasons for your answer.

4 'The only thing that really matters is feeling and living what you believe' (line 113). Do you agree with this? Are there any social problems that you feel so opposed to that you would take positive action to try to publicise the wrong?

THE HUMAN FACTOR

1 Sarah asks Maurice, 'Has something happened?' because he always phoned her when he was going to be late home and this time he did not. (2 marks)

2 Maurice says that there is nothing of consequence wrong and implies that the bad weather is to blame for his mood. (2 marks)

3 The ways in which Maurice shows that he is upset are:
   he is late home without warning Sarah
   he asks for a larger than usual whisky with no soda
   he asks untypically for another drink
   he gets into an argument with Sarah (4 marks)

4 We can discover the following points about the relationship between Maurice and Sarah:
   they have a very close relationship
   they have a very loving relationship
   they rarely quarrel
   they have a very trusting relationship (4 marks)

5 Maurice works as an agent for the Secret Service. This is his official job. (1 mark)

6 Maurice 'rates a life-time in jail' because he has become a double agent. He stole 'Muller's notes' and sent a copy of them to Halliday. (3 marks)

7 Davis was supposed to have died of excessive drinking. (1 mark)

8 'They' are Maurice's bosses in the Secret Service – government officials. (2 marks)

9 The three phrases mean:
   they had guaranteed lasting love to each other
   a presentiment of death
   concedes more than he should in an exchange. (6 marks)

THE BLEEDING HEART

1 Newton and Cambridge are miles away in culture from each other for the following reasons:
   Newton:
      is a choice white suburb
      has good schools
      has well-to-do families
   Cambridge:
      is ethnically mixed
      has people from a range of social backgrounds. (5 marks)

2 The late 60's were a time of:
      contention between races
      propaganda from different groups
      violence
      drug taking
   All these factors helped to change Elspeth. (4 marks)

3 Selene's attitude to Elspeth's mother is that she is:
      suspicious of her
      always assessing her
      always trying to get the better of her (3 marks)

4 The 'puberty rite' or adolescent ritual that Elspeth is carrying out is the shoplifting of goods she could not use. (2 marks)

5 The two examples of bigotry in the school administration are:
      they turned a blind eye to attacks on black children by white children
      they differentiated between the language expected from 'nice' white girls and black girls. (2 marks)

6 The narrator took her family to the Cape to get Elspeth away from the unsavoury atmosphere of Cambridge. (1 mark)

7 Elspeth thought her Mother was trying to destroy her relationship with Connie because she took her away from Cambridge and wouldn't allow Connie to go with them to the Cape. (2 marks)

8 The words as used in the passage mean:
      different races
      envelop
      expressionless
      machine
      apathetic
      scowled (6 marks)

INSIDE RAMPTON

1 The two things which show that Rampton is different from most other buildings are:
    the large numbers of keys
    the nurse who guards the keys.   (2 marks)
2 The lines mean that: Rampton is where society's misfits, the rubbish, are deposited. The door shuts them in as the lid of a dustbin encloses garbage.   (2 marks)
3 The punishments the three 'disturbed' girls received are:
    they were kept in solitary confinement
    they were not let out of their rooms at the same time as the other 'girls'.   (2 marks)
4 The night nurse had to check the rooms of the three girls who had been locked in the previous day as one of her duties.   (1 mark)
5 The first duties of the day shift sister are to:
    read the night nurse's report
    read about the drugs given
    count all the inmates
    sign that they are all there
    count all her staff.   (5 marks)
6 Sister Simpson accuses society of hypocrisy because society demands that these 'disturbed' people be locked up and then says 'poor things', but if they are released society objects and demands that they be sent back to Rampton.   (3 marks)
7 Young nurses are very vulnerable in Rampton because they:
    have little experience
    find it hard to understand the patients.   (2 marks)
8 The sister tries to encourage her patients by:
    telling them about her own life
    trying to give them a picture of the world outside
    trying to make them see that it is worth making an effort to get released.   (3 marks)
9 The words as used in the passage mean:
    final
    deadened, tranquillized
    far below normal intelligence
    incurable
    rejected, excluded   (5 marks)

KNIGHTS OF THE NEW YORK SUBWAY

1 The territories which the Magnificent Thirteen patrol are:
    the worst routes
    the most poorly lit stations
    the most dangerous areas.   (3 marks)
2 Their work could be described as:
    unpaid
    dangerous
    generous.   (3 marks)
3 They began their patrols because:
    trouble had escalated on the subway
    the public were terrorised by mounting violence.   (2 marks)
4 Sliwa's long-term plan is to rid Central Park of thugs and villains   (1 mark)
5 Sliwa and the others helped the inhabitants of the area in which their office is situated by getting rid of the rubbish and by ameliorating the area.   (2 marks)
6 As Sliwa and the group members wait at the tunstile they watch for fare-jumpers, possible muggers and their victims.   (2 marks)
7 Sliwa and his comrades are in stark contrast to the Transit Cop because he carries arms. Sliwa and the others carry no weapons, rely on their sharp reactions and their reputation/ presence.   (4 marks)
8 When the train arrives in a station they:
    make their way to the door
    look for the red berets of their group
    If one is missing they race to find where the trouble is.   (3 marks)
9 The words as used in the passage mean:
    damp underground   (2 marks)
    channel
    attractive
    possible   (3 marks)

MULTIPLE CHOICE COMPREHENSION
ANSWERS

THE FILM STAR
1C 2A 3B 4A 5B 6B 7D 8B 9D 10B
11D 12B 13D 14B

THE PROBLEM THAT DOESN'T GO AWAY
1A 2D 3B 4C 5B 6B 7C 8D 9B 10A
11B 12A 13A 14B 15D 16B 17A 18A 19C
20A

FLIGHT
1C 2A 3B 4D 5A 6C 7D 8D 9B 10A
11A 12C 13C 14B 15D 16A 17C 18B 19A
20D

WHEN BLACK TURNS WHITE
1D 2B 3D 4A 5B 6C 7B 8A 9C 10B
11C 12A 13B 14B 15D 16C 17D 18C 19A
20B